29.95

‖‖‖ SO-ATE-965 ‖‖‖

In Defence of
Christianity

In Defence of
Christianity

Brian Hebblethwaite

OXFORD
UNIVERSITY PRESS

OXFORD
UNIVERSITY PRESS

Great Clarendon Street, Oxford OX2 6DP

Oxford University Press is a department of the University of Oxford.
It furthers the University's objective of excellence in research, scholarship,
and education by publishing worldwide in

Oxford New York

Auckland Cape Town Dar es Salaam Hong Kong Karachi
Kuala Lumpur Madrid Melbourne Mexico City Nairobi
New Delhi Shanghai Taipei Toronto

With offices in

Argentina Austria Brazil Chile Czech Republic France Greece
Guatemala Hungary Italy Japan Poland Portugal Singapore
South Korea Switzerland Thailand Turkey Ukraine Vietnam

Oxford is a registered trade mark of Oxford University Press
in the UK and in certain other countries

British Library Cataloguing in Publication Data

Data available

Library of Congress Cataloging in Publication Data

Data to follow

Typeset by SPI Publisher Services, Pondicherry, India
Printed in Great Britain by
Biddles Ltd., King's Lynn

ISBN 0 19 927679-X   978-0-19-927679-0

1 3 5 7 9 10 8 6 4 2

For Don Cupitt

Preface

This short book of apologetics originated in the two Gifford Lectures which I contributed to a joint series in Glasgow in September 2001 and the four Hensley Henson Lectures which I delivered in Oxford in May 2002. Much rewriting and reordering has taken place, but Chapter 1 and parts of Chapters 2 and 5 were, in their original form, the two Giffords. As such, they were published as Chapters 9 and 10 of *The Nature and Limits of Human Understanding*, ed. Anthony J. Sanford (London and New York: T. & T. Clark/Continuum, 2003). This material is reused with the permission of the publisher and the University of Glasgow. Most of the rest of the book originated in the unpublished Hensons. The emphasis in Chapters 3, 4 and 6 on 'the appeal to history as an integral part of Christian apologetics' reflects the terms of Bishop Henson's bequest in founding the lectures that bear his name.

I am very grateful to the Faculties of Divinity and Theology in the Universities of Glasgow and Oxford and to colleagues and friends at those institutions for their hospitality and encouragement during my visits.

BRIAN HEBBLETHWAITE
June 2004

Contents

1

A Case for Theism

My intention in this book is to set out some of the reasoning that can be used in support of the Christian faith. I am well aware that reason is not the basis of faith. Christian faith is not founded on arguments. Most believers have either grown up and been nurtured in what have been called 'convictional communities'[1] and have simply found that religious faith and participation in religious life make sense to them, or else have been precipitated into religious commitment and practice by some powerful conversion experience. Few people are actually reasoned into faith. The arguments which I intend to sketch here are more like buttresses than foundations, reasons that can be given, as I say, in support of faith.

In this first chapter I shall draw attention to a number of wide-ranging considerations, in no way presupposing faith, which nevertheless do, cumulatively, suggest that theism— that is, belief in God—offers the best explanation of the world in which we find ourselves. (To that extent, these arguments are not restricted to the support of Christianity. Our Jewish, Muslim, Sikh, and many of our Hindu friends could appeal to them just as well.) Again, I have to admit that Christian belief, or indeed any other form of theistic belief, is not ordinarily accepted just because it explains things. But,

A Case for Theism

I repeat, the fact that such explanations do not form faith's basis in no way entails disparagement of the claim that faith can find support from the argument that theism does indeed provide the best explanation of our world.

Christianity, like all theistic faiths, includes a strong element of metaphysical thinking. Indeed, its more theoretical side cannot seriously dispense with a thoroughly metaphysical world-view. But what do I mean by metaphysics? The two main considerations leading to metaphysical thinking are, in the first place, recognition of aspects of our world left unexplained by the natural and human sciences, and, secondly, the human mind's insistent drive to think holistically, to try to make sense of, and to relate to each other, all the main aspects of our world and our experience. In fact, one could define metaphysics as such holistic thinking.

It needs to be pointed out at once that those who reject the view that there are aspects of the world left unexplained, at least in principle, by the natural and the human sciences are themselves thinking metaphysically. Materialists, or physicalists, are metaphysicians, attempting to think holistically, making large claims about everything. I shall shortly give reasons for thinking them not very good metaphysicians. But materialism is certainly metaphysics, not science.

P. F. Strawson has familiarized us with the distinction between revisionary metaphysics and descriptive metaphysics.[2] The former, revisionary metaphysics, are large-scale 'constructive' world-views (although the term 'constructive' needs qualification, since human constructions can lead to discoveries), examples being the philosophies of Plato, Leibniz, Hegel, and Whitehead. The latter, descriptive metaphysics, restrict themselves to laying bare the conceptual scheme presupposed by, or displayed in, our actual practices, whether of everyday life or of science, examples here being Aristotle (some of the time, at any rate), Kant, Strawson himself, and Michael Dummett. That Dummett can be so classified is clear from his book *The Logical Basis of Metaphysics*, where he shows how a realist metaphysics is implied by the logic of our ordinary language.[3] Indeed, the older linguistic philosophy, so anti-metaphysical in temper, is in fact full of metaphysical implications. For example, J. L. Austin's famous paper, 'Ifs and Cans',[4] with its powerful refutation of conditional analyses of our uses of the word 'can' and its correlative demonstration of the categorical nature of such uses, is highly pertinent to the metaphysics of freedom, to be considered later in this chapter.

The limitations of scientific thinking are well brought out in Ian Barbour's *Religion in an Age of Science*[5] and in John Barrow's *Theories of Everything*.[6] These authors have shown that neither in fact nor in logic could a 'Grand Unified Theory' such as Einstein sought, or a 'Theory of Everything' such as Hawking proposes, ever predict or explain the capacity of the world stuff, if I may crudely call it that, to come up with life and consciousness, let alone mind, freedom, and morality, and all the products of intelligence, insight, and creativity in philosophy and culture generally. It would, no doubt, be a remarkable scientific achievement, well worthy of a Nobel Prize, to come up with a theory of everything. Its expressibility in a single mathematical equation would be highly impressive. But it would not enable us to predict or explain any of the features of the world that I have just listed.

Reductionism in biology and sociobiology fares no better than reductionism in physics. Here I refer to John Eccles's *The Human Mystery*,[7] Arthur Peacocke's *Theology for a Scientific*

Age,[8] and John Polkinghorne's *Science and Christian Belief.*[9] One does not have to be an expert to follow these authors in claiming that Richard Dawkins's account of altruism, E. O. Wilson's account of culture, and P. M. Churchland's account of what he calls 'folk psychology' do not begin to account for, or do justice to, human love, human knowledge, including scientific knowledge, or human creativity as exemplified in Dante, Shakespeare, and Goethe.

Cognitive science has been held to pose the greatest threat to the autonomy of these domains, which, I am suggesting, resist reductionism and demand metaphysical explanation. But again, one does not have to be an expert to see that the word 'information' in 'information technology' is being used in a purely metaphorical sense, or to agree with Peter Geach that 'machines manifestly have no life, no sense, no feeling, no purposes except their maker's'. 'It is a suitable nemesis of human pride', says Geach, 'that men should be getting ready to perform acts of brutish idolatry—to humble themselves before the superior minds that they, like the heathen before them, believe they can get to inhabit inanimate artefacts.'[10]

This brings me to the topic of consciousness and the metaphysical questions raised by this phenomenon. The implausibility of scientific reductionism at this point is particularly striking. This goes for Hume's give-away reference to 'this little agitation of the brain which we call thought', for Darwin's equally give-away reference to thought as 'a secretion of the brain', and for the contemporary attempts of such scholars as Crick, Dennett, Chalmers, and even Edelman to give a purely physicalist or biological account of consciousness. The irreducibility of consciousness, and *a fortiori* of mind, and their basality as facts of nature have been well brought out by

John Searle in his *The Mystery of Consciousness* and other works,[11] and, from a more Wittgensteinian perspective, by Anthony Kenny in *The Metaphysics of Mind*.[12] I will concentrate here on Searle's position. For Searle, it is a fact of nature that evolution has produced developed organisms with brains that, somehow, give rise to consciousness. This experienced fact rules out pure physicalism. The fact that the stuff of the world has the capacity to evolve consciousness shows that there is more to matter or energy than those aspects of nature studied in physics. But Searle rejects any resort to mind–body dualism. 'We can accept irreducibility...without accepting dualism,' he says. In this he would be supported not only by Kenny, but also by Polkinghorne, who insists that we are talking about one world, with all its amazing capacities and powers to evolve consciousness, mind and all the products of mind.

In the end I hope to be able to stay with this one-world-view, if I can. But I have to say that the case for dualism is stronger than Searle allows. The arguments of H. D. Lewis in *The Elusive Mind*,[13] of Richard Swinburne in *The Evolution of the Soul*,[14] and of Karl Popper and John Eccles in *The Self and its Brain*[15] are strong arguments. They take into account features of our experience as agents and thinkers which get less than adequate attention in Searle's extended naturalism. Searle refers at one point to Eccles's religious commitment to the existence of a soul, but this does not do justice to the arguments actually used for dualism. Popper, of course, has no such religious commitment, and I have found no discussion of Popper's views in Searle's writings. Swinburne's arguments, in *The Evolution of the Soul*, are purely philosophical arguments and, while Swinburne's mind–body dualism does play a pivotal role in his overall defence of theism, it is not itself a product of his theistic metaphysics. Polkinghorne's theistic world-view, as I have already noted, is resolutely anti-dualistic, as is that of many contemporary Christian theologians. Clearly there is no necessary link between religious commitment and mind–body dualism.

This matter of religious, or indeed non-religious, presuppositions deserves some reflection. Philosophers tend to be coy about this, except when writing off views coming from an explicitly religious source. One recalls Bertrand Russell's totally inadequate treatment of Thomas Aquinas in his *History of Western Philosophy.*[16] Alvin Plantinga, of course, is anything but coy. His 'Advice to Christian Philosophers' was precisely that they should have confidence in the import of their theistic world-view on the central problems of philosophy.[17] In this book, I shall be urging that a theistic metaphysics makes most sense of the world as we know it to be. On the other side, Derek Parfit is one of the few secular philosophers who urge a comparable confidence in bringing out the implications of atheism. At the end of his *Reasons and Persons*[18] he points out that, since disbelief in God is relatively recent, non-religious ethics is at a very early stage. Not surprisingly, he acknowledges a similarity between his own atheistic view of persons and that of early, non-theistic Buddhism.

Certainly one should be alert to the question of the bearing of one's theistic or non-theistic perspective on the whole mind–body problem. And no assumptions should be made, without scrutiny, about the benignity or malignity of such influences either way. But since, as I say, there is no necessary connection between theism and dualism, or between anti-dualism and atheism, I propose to concentrate here on the factors themselves that require to be reckoned with in any plausible metaphysics of consciousness and the mind.

Searle's non-reductive view of consciousness as a basic datum of experience and his hypothesis that consciousness is somehow caused by the brain may be taken as starting-points for our discussion. But the *sui generis* nature of consciousness is not very well brought out by comparison with supervenient properties such as liquidity, which cannot be reduced simply to the movement of water molecules. Moreover, *qualia*, that is, the experienced states of awareness on the part of conscious beings such as ourselves, while they are indeed, in some unknown manner, the product of brains in receipt of external and internal data, are nevertheless themselves causally efficacious, not only in respect of behaviour, as Searle acknowledges, but also in respect of the neural firings which accompany behaviour. The case for mind–body interactionism is very strong. If, for example, I say that I will demonstrate the power of mind over matter by raising my arm after a count of five, it is my conscious intention to prove the point that brings about the movement of my arm, and, presumably, the complex neural firings in my brain, and what occurs between my brain and my arm to make it go up. This example brings out the further point that we are not just talking about different types of properties, physical and mental, that the natural world contains. It is not just a question of mental states supervening upon brain states. What we are talking about is human subjectivity, the conscious and self-conscious ownership of one's mental states, one's sensations, one's thoughts, one's intentions, and one's actions.

The self or person, far from being just a bundle of perceptions, as Hume famously called it,[19] to his own very proper dissatisfaction, possesses what Kant called a 'transcendental unity of apperception'.[20] But we have to say more about this than Kant felt able to say. As an individual human being, I am much more than an animal organism with a unique perspective. As a subject, a self, an agent, a person in relation to other persons (I am deliberately echoing the language of John Macmurray's Gifford Lectures here[21]), I transcend my physical and biological base. And metaphysics has to do justice to this transcendence. It is not simply a matter of my mental states initiating changes in my physical states, as in raising my arm to prove a point; it is I, *qua* conscious and acting subject, who bring about these changes.

Our ignorance about how all this works is very great. One is all too conscious of the limits of human understanding at this point. We are familiar with the idea of 'apophaticism', our inability to say what God is, in theology. But the secular mind has no business mocking the doctrine of divine incomprehensibility, when so much ignorance about earthly matters has to be acknowledged. Apophaticism is as rampant in science and philosophy as it is in theology. John Searle admits that we do not know how the brain causes consciousness. *A fortiori*, we do not know how consciousness causes physical movement, including neural firing. We do not know how a higher animal organism with a developed brain becomes a conscious thinking subject and a free agent.

But just as apophaticism in theology need not, and should not, prevent us from saying *something* about God and God's relation to the world, so our ignorance about the mind–brain relation need not, and should not, prevent us from exploring that relation and coming up with, admittedly highly tentative, hypotheses concerning the nature of a universe that has it in it to evolve consciousness and to evolve persons. This will inevitably take us beyond science into metaphysics.

In no way am I ignoring the progress made by neurophysiologists in locating the correlations between brain states, on the one hand, and thoughts and intentions and language capacities, on the other. But the scope for misinterpreting these results is very great. In a recent television programme on these matters, a certain philosopher seemed to be suggesting that the discovery that her decision to press a certain key was preceded by, not just correlated with, a set of neural firings showed that the decision was brought about by physical processes in the brain. But this conclusion is quite unwarranted. Any actual decision is going to be preceded not only by reflection but also by largely unconscious ranging over the possibilities. All of this will of course be accompanied by and correlated with, but surely not just brought about by, the appropriate neural firings.

I should perhaps give some reasons why I am reluctant to embrace mind–body dualism, despite my conviction of the *sui generis* nature not only of consciousness, but also of the mind, the self, persons in relation, and the cultural products of human intelligence and creativity. There are three main reasons why I prefer to stick to a one-world metaphysics, provided full justice is done to all aspects of this one world. In the first place, we have to reckon with the lower forms of consciousness. I do not know at what point consciousness appears, either in evolution or in the hierarchy of living beings. But, clearly, plants are not conscious, whereas animals are. There is a threshold here which undoubtedly gets crossed, just as there is a threshold between inanimate and living beings. But the fact of lowly degrees of consciousness, say in insects or fish, makes it implausible to suppose that we are talking of a *separate* mental substance when we enter the realm of consciousness.

This brings me to my second reason for avoiding dualism. We now know so much about the dependency of consciousness upon brain activity (I have agreed with Searle that, as far as products of evolution are concerned, and that includes ourselves, brains cause consciousness) that the idea of mind as a separate substance is difficult to sustain. The reality of consciousness is part of the world's reality. We need an ontology of nature comprehensive enough to include its capacity to evolve life, consciousness, intelligence, and selfhood. Not that the idea of pure mind or pure spirit, unconnected with a material base in an evolved nervous system, is a complete nonsense. No theist could hold that. A more basic dualism between God and the world is still defensible. And God is incorporeal Spirit. Later, I shall be arguing that an infinite creative mind and will makes better sense of the created world's capacity to evolve minds and selves. But created minds and selves are best thought of as built up from below, in and through nature.

My third reason for avoiding dualism is in fact a theological reason. One of the oddities of Swinburne's book is that, while he believes that the soul is correlated with a certain complex organism on whose operation it depends, at least for the time being, for its conscious functioning, he nevertheless postulates its special creation as a separate substance at a certain stage of physical and biological development, both in the course of evolution and in the course of each animal's and human embryo's growth.[22] Surely creation is better thought of as the calling into being of a universe of energies endowed from the beginning with the capacity and power to come up with the conditions of life and to evolve consciousness, minds, and persons.

A Case for Theism

From this one-world perspective, I have to put a question mark against Karl Popper's talk of three worlds. Popper speaks of 'World 1' as the world of physical reality, 'World 2' as the world of mental states and acts, and 'World 3' as the world of the linguistic, intellectual, and cultural products of 'World 2' activity.[23] Without denying the reality of what Popper is classifying, I think we should see these as three aspects or elements in the one world, all of them requiring attention and explanation in any plausible metaphysics. As for Roger Penrose's three worlds, the physical, the mental, and the mathematical,[24] a view which Searle ascribes to Penrose's Platonist metaphysics, I prefer to reinterpret this, as I do towards the end of this chapter, in terms of the rational structure of the one created world reflecting the rationality and mind of its Maker, God.

Let me add a further point about the capacity of this one world to evolve minds. It is a point often made, but it is worth repeating. The sheer size of the universe is no reason to depreciate the significance of the evolution of mind in one tiny corner of one solar system in one galaxy among myriads. The quantitative dimensions of the physical base of the evolution of life, consciousness, and intelligence are totally irrelevant to the question of the significance of these qualitative developments. And it seems to be the case anyway, as cosmologists driven to posit some anthropic principle point out,[25] that such a vast field of energy is a necessary condition for the cosmic evolution of conditions stable and fruitful enough for the thresholds into life, consciousness, and mind to be able to be crossed anywhere. Of course, there is much debate as to whether this is likely to have happened many times, in our own galaxy or in distant galaxies, or only once here on Earth. I am inclined to think that belief in extraterrestrial intelligent life reflects secular prejudice.

A Case for Theism

The arguments in its favour are purely statistical, whereas the empirical evidence points to uniqueness. Not only is there no evidence for extraterrestrial intelligent life,[26] purely statistical probabilities are outweighed by the extraordinary number of improbable coincidences that have to obtain before the thresholds in question can be crossed. One cannot argue simply from the evident capacity of the world stuff to evolve minds that it must have done so in many places and at many times.

But my present point is that, whether the universe has in fact evolved minds many times or only once, the appearance of the noosphere, to use Teilhard de Chardin's term,[27] is a qualitative leap of vast significance, given its nature and its results, quite irrespective of the sheer size of the mindless universe out of which it has appeared.

I now turn to freedom and morality, two major, and of course linked, elements in this new significant dimension, the noosphere, of this one evolving world. What we have to try to make sense of, in our holistic metaphysical thinking, is the capacity of the world stuff to evolve not only consciousness and mind, but free beings and moral persons and communities.

Again, with Searle, I take it as a basic datum of our experience as human beings that we are free. Our freedom of thought and action is far more certain than the alleged results of any piece of rational argument or scientific research. The very processes of rational argument and scientific research themselves presuppose our freedom. Arguments in defence of the freedom of the will, in so far as they are needed, have been set out by Austin Farrer in *The Freedom of the Will*[28] and by John Lucas in his *The Freedom of the Will.*[29] Lucas's use of Gödel's theorem to show the impossibility of giving an account of our thinking in such a way as formally to include recognition of its own validity has been widely discussed but never refuted. Obituaries of Elizabeth Anscombe referred to her alleged demolition of C. S. Lewis's presentation of an informal version of this argument. But, as Michael Dummett pointed out,[30] Lewis was far from decisively refuted. He returned with a refined version of the argument,[31] and Anscombe herself subscribed to a version of it in her own inaugural lecture at Cambridge.[32] It has received a powerful restatement by Stephen Clark in his *God, Religion and Reality*.[33] Briefly, the argument goes like this: if a belief of mine is simply the determined outcome of chemical processes in my brain, then there is no way of judging whether or not it is true.

The point of such arguments, formal or informal, is to bring out the fact of our freedom of thought, our ability to range freely, in thought, over relevant considerations, to weigh evidence and arguments, and to reach responsible conclusions as to where the truth lies or where it probably lies. Lewis was accused of confusing reasons and causes, but in fact, reasons are a species of cause in a wide sense of cause; although they effect things in a very different way from, say, chemical processes operating willy-nilly. In particular, they are not determining causes. They do not compel their effects. They provide sufficient conditions, not in the sense that, given these conditions, the effect is bound to occur, but rather in the sense that, given these conditions, the effect, whether a belief or an action, makes most sense and is seen to be justified and thus likely to be held or to be done.

All this, as I say, applies to both thought and action. Where action is concerned, our freedom and responsibility are presupposed by our whole form of life as individuals and as members of society. While this is most evident in the moral sphere, all our language of praise and blame, the whole institution of reward and punishment, presupposing freedom and responsibility, it is also true of more humdrum choices, such as which book to read or which friend to visit. And I stress again that the activities of scientific research themselves cannot be explained deterministically.

Clearly there are degrees of freedom, and it is interesting to enquire at what point in evolution, or in the life history of a child, rudimentary freedom becomes a reality. Not even animal behaviour, at least that of the higher animals, can be accounted for wholly in terms of stimulus and response.

Metaphysical questions arise over how it can be the case that organisms succeed in evolving these capacities and powers. Again I refer to Anscombe's recognition that, while indeterminacy is not the same as freedom, it may well be 'the physical correlate of human freedom of action, and perhaps also of the voluntariness and intentionalness of the conduct of other animals'.[34] Certainly the indeterminacy of quantum physics and chaos theory has made it much easier to see that the physical universe does possess the flexibility and openness required for the emergence of autonomous beings, able to take control of things and shape the future for themselves in the spheres of both thought and action.

That freedom and morality are linked needs little argument. 'Ought' implies 'can'. Kant's second postulate of practical reason—his insistence, that is, that our being subject to the moral law necessarily implies our freedom—is seldom questioned even by those who do question his first and third postulates: immortality and God.[35] But equally, 'can' implies 'ought'. It is our freedom that opens up to us the moral dimensions of responsibility and choice between good and evil. But how are we to understand this moral sphere? Is it just a matter of subjective and intersubjective preference? Or do we, as Kant thought, find ourselves subject to moral constraints and demands by the very nature of things? Kant's conviction of the categorical nature of the moral law was the linchpin of his whole philosophy. As Allen Wood has shown,[36] Kant's critical philosophy cannot be understood if we fail to take seriously his conviction that a strict delimitation of theoretical understanding was necessary in order to make room for moral faith. Moral faith, for Kant, involved not only recognition of the demands of the moral law; it also involved drawing out the implications of the fact that we exist under its constraints. This is where all three postulates of practical reason come in. The postulates of immortality and God were required not simply to explain the realizability of the highest good. They were required as necessary conditions of the universe in which we find ourselves being, despite appearances, a moral universe.

Kant made discussion of these matters very difficult for himself by his insistence on the inaccessibility of the noumenal world, the world as it is in itself, to theoretical understanding. His immediate successors in German Idealism soon breached these boundaries. And in our own day, as I have already indicated, moralists have less to fear from post-Newtonian science, which lacks the rigid deterministic implications of Newton's world-view. Also, I do not think that we have to restrict ourselves to Kant's own rigid epistemology. Our conceptual framework is a much more flexible product of continual interaction with a real world environment; and our reflection on experience is capable of much greater analogical extension in speculative metaphysics than Kant allowed. In fact, Kant's own practice, in moral philosophy, in teleology, and in philosophical theology, went much further in spelling out the necessary conditions of this being a moral universe than his strict epistemology would allow.

Be that as it may, I now want to introduce the names of two more recent philosophers who have explored the implications of the objectivity of morals in the interest of a wider metaphysics: Iris Murdoch and Donald MacKinnon. Murdoch's Gifford Lectures, *Metaphysics as a Guide to Morals*,[37] could equally well have been entitled *Morals as a Guide to Metaphysics*. Not that she actually develops a metaphysical world-view that tries to make sense of the good and the beautiful as objective realities, basic to the nature of things. But her Platonic insistence on the Good as a transcendent object of attention and love is very striking. 'We *experience*', she writes,

both the reality of perfection and its distance away, and this leads us to place our idea of it outside the world of existent being as something of a different unique and special sort. Such experience of the reality of good is not like an arbitrary and assertive resort to our own will; it is a discovery of something independent of us, where that independence is essential.[38]

Murdoch herself would not accept a theistic interpretation of the objectivity of the Good, since, for her, a god could only be an existent object among other objects, and she shared the modern demythologizing attitude to such allegedly supernatural entities. She endorsed Don Cupitt's 'taking leave' of God in this sense, but not his extreme anti-realism. That simply failed to do justice, she thought, to our moral experience of the objectivity and transcendence of the Good.

It has to be said that Murdoch's position is deeply obscure. No one has succeeded in explaining the ontological status of her objective Good as the transcendent object of attention, any more than Plato's. As I shall be arguing, Neoplatonism's theistic reinterpretation of Plato was a necessary development, if sense was to be made of the objectivity of goodness and beauty. But that involved a theism that precisely did not see God as just the supreme object among other objects in an inventory of the furniture of the world. All the same, I take Murdoch's insistence on the objectivity of value as a pointer in the direction of a metaphysics broad enough to make sense of a universe that has not only evolved consciousness and minds and free persons in relation, but beings capable of discerning goodness, beauty, and truth. And what they discern at this high point of evolutionary development are dimensions of reality way beyond the physical, chemical, and biological base from which such discernments have evolved. Unlike Murdoch, I shall be arguing that a theistic metaphysics makes most sense of all this.

I insert at this point a note on Don Cupitt's inability to sustain a purely subjectivist, expressivist, anti-realist approach. Having previously endorsed postmodernism's deconstruction of every kind of metaphysical realism, in a more recent book[39] he found himself driven to admit that language cannot be the whole story. There must be something given, which language forms into our human world. He calls this something 'being', with reference to Heidegger, though in a sense remote from the latter's highly obscure existentialist ontology. Often Cupitt deliberately writes 'be-ing' with a hyphen, to indicate its dynamic, wholly unformed nature, until language clothes it with ever changing forms. How strange that Cupitt's return to metaphysics should come about this way! He now finds himself postulating something not unlike the pre-Socratic Anaximander's 'unlimited' or 'indefinite': that is, the formless matter of a world yet to be shaped up, in Anaximander's case by separating out of opposites, in Cupitt's case by human language. We are right back, then, at the very beginnings of Western metaphysics with an obscure, primitive theory that explains nothing. Indeed, Cupitt's new-found metaphysics is even more opaque than Anaximander's; for why on earth suppose that it is human language that gives form to the basic stuff of the world and to the natural kinds that we discover in the universe and here on Earth?

Returning to the theme of how moral philosophy implies a metaphysics of transcendence, I now cite the work of Donald MacKinnon, and in particular his Gifford Lectures, *The Problem of Metaphysics*.[40] The burden of those lectures, worked out with typical earnestness and agonizing over the import of tragedy and parable, was that 'in moral experience transcendence is present to us all along'.[41] MacKinnon saw in Kant's doctrine of the primacy of practical reason the classical expression of the approach which sees the metaphysical as 'something that presses on us with a directness and immediacy which requires no argument to convince us of its reality'. And he adds here, in a footnote, 'It is the analysis of this pressure that constitutes the crux of this whole book.' The parables of Jesus are analysed by MacKinnon as paradigmatic examples of the way in which we have to do with perception of how things are. And similarly, the tragedies of Sophocles and Shakespeare are called upon to demonstrate our discontent with any kind of naturalism. 'It is', MacKinnon writes, 'as if we are constrained in pondering the extremities of human life to acknowledge the transcendent as the only alternative to the kind of trivialisation which would empty of significance the sort of experience with which we have been concerned'[42]—that is, in exploring the significance of *Antigone* and *Lear*.

Let me try to put the argument a little more straightforwardly. The point at issue is the way in which moral facts point ineluctably to transcendence. When confronted with the moral law or with the moral significance of human life in situations of tragedy or of supreme goodness or radical evil, we find ourselves unable to subscribe to a naturalistic philosophy of value as no more than intersubjective preference. And we have to try to make metaphysical sense of an evolving world that has come to manifest such values. Obviously, one has to admit that moral facts are difficult to comprehend. One of J. L. Mackie's main arguments for the subjectivity of morals in his book *Ethics: Inventing Right and Wrong*[43] was 'the argument from queerness'. Objective values are very queer entities. So they are, from a naturalistic perspective. But given the pressures to admit them, pressures which we have seen articulated by Kant, Murdoch, and MacKinnon, we are driven to question the naturalistic perspective. As I shall be arguing, a theistic metaphysics makes most sense of these otherwise queer facts. Ironically, Mackie admits this hypothetically—that is, if we could embrace theism, which Mackie himself could not. But the unacceptability of naturalism, its trivialization of moral experience, should make us look again at the question of the coherence of theism, too easily dismissed by Mackie.

This argument is structurally similar to the argument from truth which I have used elsewhere.[44] In brief: Nietzsche's aphorism that, with the death of God, truth becomes fiction falls foul of our obstinate conviction that truth is a matter of discovery, not invention. This is best accounted for on the supposition of a Creator God who has given the world its discoverable reality and sustains it.

I now turn to the indubitable fact that this evolving universe has come up, not only with consciousness, mind, freedom, and moral value, but also with great art and culture, yet more profound and objective values, this time in the sphere of beauty. The question now is: how are we to make sense of a universe capable of manifesting the beautiful and the sublime, as well as evolving beings capable of sublime artistic creativity, of coming up, that is, with Dante, Shakespeare, and Goethe?

The spheres of morality and aesthetics are clearly linked, as MacKinnon's wrestling with *Antigone* and *Lear* shows. But beauty is a dimension of the real that includes many more facets than those seen in surpassing goodness or confronted in the depths of tragedy. Natural beauty, comedy (I think of play as one of the sociologist Peter Berger's 'signals of transcendence'[45]), the heights and depths of musical composition, the serenity of a Claude landscape, or the teasing ambiguities of Poussin's *A Dance to the Music of Time*, the exquisite cadences of poetic expression (George Steiner cites Shakespeare's 'There sleeps Titania sometime of the night' from *A Midsummer Night's Dream*)—all these wonders resist the subjectivist proverb about beauty being in the eye of the beholder and give substance to Keats's conclusion to his *Ode on a Grecian Urn*: 'Beauty is truth, truth beauty—that is all/Ye know on earth and all ye need to know.' Bernard Levin wrote of Shakespeare: 'The ultimate wonder of Shakespeare is the deep, sustaining realisation that his work, in addition to all its other qualities— poetical, dramatic, philosophical, psychological—is above all true.'[46] But what kind of truth? The whole burden of objectivism in aesthetic theory, an objectivism which, like ethical objectivism, will not go away, is that what we perceive in the beauty of nature and the sublimities of artistic creation is something of the true nature of things.

Such reflections have informed such major strands in the history of philosophy as Platonism, German Idealism, and Romanticism, to which we shall be turning in a moment. Schopenhauer, Schelling and Hegel all saw music and art as representations of the infinite. For Hegel, artistic beauty reveals absolute truth through perception.[47] Of course, the fact that art yields metaphysical knowledge in sensual form does, for Hegel, mean that art must be transcended by religion, just as religion must be transcended by philosophy, if conceptual knowledge of the Absolute is to be attained. This progress from art, through religion, to philosophy will be questioned shortly. But, clearly, Hegel had a higher view of the cognitive significance of art than, say, R. G. Collingwood, for whom the figments of the imagination that constitute art only hint at the realities discovered and experienced in religion.[48]

For much of modernity and postmodernity all this has been lost sight of. Few secular philosophers now would be disposed to affirm the metaphysical significance of great art. Yet, as I say, the objective value of beauty, like cheerfulness, keeps breaking in. This has seldom been better expressed in the context of our own current cultural situation than by George Steiner, who, in his book *Real Presences*, asks us to reconsider the assumption 'that all serious art and literature, and not only music to which Nietzsche applies the term, is an *opus metaphysicum*'.[49] Steiner gives many examples, including examples from Dante and Shakespeare, where this assumption is virtually forced upon us. But his prime examples come from music. Music, he says 'has long been . . . the unwritten theology of those who lack or reject any formal creed'. And he asks us just to listen to the slow movement of Schubert's C major Quintet. I shall return to this kind of insight in a moment. But, in summary, Steiner extends his argument to cover all great art. I quote him at some length here:

It is, I believe, poetry, art and music which relate us most directly to that in being which is not ours. Science is no less animate in its making of models and images. But these are not, finally, disinterested. They aim at mastery, at ownership. It is counter-creation and counter-love, as these are embodied in the aesthetic and in our reception of formed meaning, which puts us in sane touch with that which transcends, with matters 'undreamt of' in our materiality... The arts are most wonderfully rooted in substance, in the human body, in stone, in pigment, in the twanging of gut or the weight of wind on reeds. All good art and literature begin in immanence. But they do not stop there. Which is to say, very plainly, that it is the enterprise and privilege of the aesthetic to quicken into lit presence the continuum between temporality and eternity, between matter and spirit, between man and 'the other'. It is in this common and exact sense that *poiesis* opens on to, is underwritten by, the religious and the metaphysical.'[50]

To return to music: it is sometimes suggested that the deep aesthetic experience of a Henry Wood Promenade Concert audience listening to a Mahler symphony in the Albert Hall, or of a Wagner audience in Bayreuth, or of a solitary individual (Inspector Morse, perhaps) listening to the Schubert C Major Quintet, is a kind of substitute for religion, providing solace and depth to the human spirit in ways religion used to do. But this fails totally to do justice to the nature and significance of what is experienced in great music, or in the poetry of Dante, Shakespeare, and Goethe, to cite those giants of European culture one again. As I have written elsewhere, 'art and culture can and should be seen not just as products of human sensibility but as clues to the meaning and worth of the whole cosmic process out of which we have evolved. It is the very nature of aesthetic, as of moral, value that belies materialism as a total world view, and provides one of the many starting-points for a cumulative argument for the existence of God.'[51]

Literary critics have long inclined towards such intimations of transcendence. In an essay on 'Goethe as the Sage',[52] T. S. Eliot writes first of the permanence and universality of figures such as Dante, Shakespeare, and Goethe, their ability to speak to successive generations and, albeit from a specific cultural background, to readers world-wide. He then writes of the abundance, amplitude, and unity of their work, its range and diversity, and the way in which it illuminates life and the world. He writes of the wisdom of these authors, a wisdom discernible and acceptable whether or not we agree with their own particular philosophical or religious views. The point is made with specific reference to Goethe; but in a much earlier essay on Dante,[53] Eliot made a similar point with reference to the Tuscan poet. We do not have to share Dante's medieval Catholicism in order to understand and appreciate the depths and heights and the sheer range of human sensibility that the *Divine Comedy* manifests. But the question that concerns us here—and again it is George Steiner who asks it most explicitly—is whether the wisdom and understanding found in, and conveyed by, poets such as Dante, Shakespeare, and Goethe are just a matter of human sensibility, however profound, or whether we do not find in such work insight into the very meaning of life and the very meaning of the world in a more transcendental sense. As Steiner puts it in his essay on Dante,[54] while adverting to the particularities of time and place in Dante's, as in Proust's, design: 'The text is timeless, universal, because utterly dated and placed. Dante and Proust, like no others, give us the gossip of eternity.' But, of course, Shakespeare and Goethe do the same.

The relation between art, metaphysics, and religion must now be considered explicitly. It can hardly be, as Hegel thought, a matter of progression from art to religion, and thence to philosophy. That gives an exaggerated significance to the conceptual. Indeed, I shall be discussing philosophy before I explore religion. But I do not wish to replace Hegel's progression with a revised progression from art, through metaphysics, to religion. For art, like morals, has itself, as Steiner shows, both metaphysical and religious significance. And if theistic metaphysics yields the best explanation for the capacities of the universe to evolve both goodness and beauty, then the best metaphysics will turn out to be an aspect of religion. But only an aspect; for the very nature of the universe, the values it has come up with in the realms of morality and art, demand practical and affective responses as well as cognitive and conceptual ones. And these are key elements in religion, which concerns itself not only with knowledge but also with love, with wonder, and with joy.

First, however, I turn to philosophy, in particular to revisionary metaphysics, to use Strawson's phrase once more. I am not only concerned to ask which strands in the history of philosophy make most sense of the phenomena of consciousness, mind, freedom, morality, and art, and of a world productive of such things. I am also concerned to ask the more Hegelian question of how best we are to understand a cosmos capable of coming up with just such philosophies, themselves, on any reckoning, remarkable constituents of Popper's 'World 3' or, better, of Polkinghorne's 'one world'.

I have already referred to Platonism and Neoplatonism as among the most fertile strands in philosophy in respect of their ability to fashion a comprehensive account of the place of mind in nature, and of the beautiful and the good as not only requiring metaphysical explanation but as affording the key ideas for metaphysical explanation. The Cambridge Platonists, and in particular Cudworth's *The True Intellectual System of the Universe*,[55] still retain great visionary power. Douglas Hedley has shown the striking congruence between Coleridge's Christian Platonism and certain strands in German Idealism.[56] As Hedley observes, 'Coleridge's metaphysics attempts to explain the "lower" (nature) in terms of that which is higher (spirit) whereas the naturalist explains the higher in terms of the lower, the spiritual realm in purely natural terms.'[57] We have already seen how Platonism recurs again and again in the philosophy of mathematics, as in Roger Penrose's work[58] or in Gödel's response to the later Bertrand Russell.[59] And the strength of Neoplatonism as a continuing tradition of holistic explanation may be seen in the aforementioned work of Stephen Clark.[60]

It may well be that Platonism fails to get the relation between nature and spirit quite right. Its weakness *vis-à-vis* the doctrine of creation is undeniable. But recognition of the ultimate dependence of nature on spirit and a preference for 'top-down' rather than 'bottom-up' explanation are features of lasting import in this tradition, as they are in seventeenth-century rationalism and in nineteenth-century German Idealism.

It is easy to criticize the great seventeenth-century rationalists for their exaggerated views of the power and scope of human reason. And it is easy to point to specific implausibilities in the systems of individual thinkers: Descartes's extreme mind–matter dualism, Malebranche's 'occasionalist' denial of causal efficacy in nature, Spinoza's pantheistic determinism, and Leibniz's 'pre-established harmony' between mind and body. But, as recent interest in, and work on, these philosophers has shown,[61] we are dealing here with minds that have seen the problems, ranged over the possibilities, debated with the ancients and the moderns, and exemplified the kind of holistic metaphysical thinking that enlarges our understanding even when we disagree. Above all, they have taken seriously the phenomena of mind and reason, their place in nature, and their transcendence of nature.

The same is true of German Idealism. I have already mentioned its breaking out from the self-imposed limitations of Kant's critical philosophy. There is much to admire in Fichte's attempt at a transcendental explanation of consciousness and experience, and his (Kantian) conviction of the basicality of freedom and the moral law. But Fichte's philosophy of nature leaves much to be desired, and, certainly for the theist, the biggest problem with Fichte is his inability to recognize the explanatory force of infinite Spirit *vis-à-vis* the contingencies of nature and finite spirit. On these grounds both Hegel and Schelling have been found more fruitful for the kind of metaphysics called for, if sense is to be made of the whole history of the world, including the spheres of mind, morals, art, philosophy, and religion under special consideration here. Recent Hegel studies by Charles Taylor,[62] Peter Hodgson,[63] and Raymond Plant,[64] to name but a few, have shown the continuing fertility and power of Hegel's all-embracing philosophy. But it is not surprising, given Hegel's (admittedly dynamic) monism, that it was Schelling's later philosophy that proved the greater influence, both on Coleridge's Christian Platonism and on Paul Tillich's theistic ontology.

Similarly, the monistic Absolute of the British Idealists gave way to the much more plausible Personal Idealism of J. R. Illingworth,[65] Hastings Rashdall,[66] and C. C. J. Webb,[67] whose theistic metaphysics still repay close study, as do those of A. E. Taylor[68] and William Temple,[69] both brought up in the Idealist tradition, but moving away from it in a more realist direction. Temple's insistence, in his *Nature, Man and God*, that the process which has led to the emergence of mind and spirit here on Earth should be evaluated in terms of its highest product, exemplifies perfectly the line of thought recommended in this chapter.

Space prevents more than a mention of process thought. But the considerations that led A. N. Whitehead away from mathematical logic to an all-embracing metaphysics of becoming are precisely those informing my present concerns.[70]

Existentialism, too, gets little more than a mention here. For all the profundity and insight of its characterization of authentic and inauthentic human existence, it fails to satisfy unless, as with Heidegger, it seeks to unfold a more general ontology, relating human being to being as such. Not that Heidegger really satisfies, given his obscurity and his wholly implausible generalizations concerning Western metaphysics as leading inexorably to the apotheosis of technology. Very little of the revisionary metaphysics cited here would fit that description. Nevertheless, the later Heidegger's depiction of poetry as the 'shepherd of Being'[71] can be taken as an obscure hint in the direction of a metaphysics of art, towards which George Steiner points, and which I endorsed as one strand in the overall world-view being sought.

As we move more and more into one world of global communication in many different spheres, economic, technological, political, and ethical (I think of Hans Küng's global ethics project at this point), we become increasingly aware of the common heritage of world philosophies, their great diversity, admittedly, but also their recurring commonalities. To read Ninian Smart's *World Philosophies*,[72] or *A Companion to World Philosophies*, in the *Blackwell Companions to Philosophy* series,[73] is to see how, again and again, out of different cultural backgrounds, the same metaphysical and epistemological questions have been addressed, often with strikingly similar results. This is especially true of the theistic world-views that have been developed out of centres in the Middle East, the Indian subcontinent, parts of Africa, and, to a certain degree, in other parts of the globe. Comparative studies by scholars such as Julius Lipner with regard to the twelfth-century Hindu theologian Ramanuja,[74] by R. C. Zaehner with regard to the twentieth-century Hindu thinker Sri Aurobindo,[75] and by Keith Ward, whose comparative theology will be discussed in Chapter 5,[76] are among the many that show the fertility and power of theistic metaphysics to make sense of a universe capable of coming up with mind, morality, art, philosophy, and religion. Of course, world philosophy includes many examples of non-theistic, sceptical, and anti-metaphysical philosophies. But the question has to be pressed: can these provide any explanation, let alone a more adequate explanation, of the data that world history and experience of being in the world thrust upon us?

Theistic metaphysics, in a number of different ways, suggests that a nature productive of finite spirit and of the values of goodness, beauty, and truth is best understood as the creation of infinite Spirit, itself supremely good, beautiful, and true, the creative act endowing the universe with its given nature, its given powers, and its ultimate meaning and destiny. Also, as I mentioned before, theistic metaphysics offers the best explanation of all the necessary features of the contingent world, its mathematical expressibility, its conformity to the laws of logic, and the properties and abstract ideas that it instantiates—all the features discerned but not explained by pure Platonism. For theistic metaphysics, mathematics and logic reflect the consistency and rationality of God's necessary being, while abstract ideas and properties are God's creative ideas. So all the necessities in the created world, and indeed in any possible world, depend on either the nature or the will of God.[77]

The two principal difficulties with such theistic metaphysics are, of course, the alleged incoherence of theism and the problem of evil. These difficulties cannot be addressed here, in a book concentrating on positive apologetic. But, clearly, the plausibility of theistic metaphysics in providing the best explanation of the world process and of the possibilities it realizes depends on at least some success in defending theism's coherence and offering a theodicy.

In singling out theistic metaphysics from the plethora of world philosophies I am already entering the field of religion. The phenomenology of religion as practised by Rudolf Otto,[78] Gerardus van der Leeuw,[79] and Ninian Smart[80] and the history of religions as practised by Ernst Troeltsch[81] and Mircea Eliade[82] yield data, including theistic metaphysics and including the theologies to be discussed in Chapter 5, which themselves provide clues to the meaning of the whole world process that has come up with such things. But I conclude this chapter by drawing attention to the other central aspects of religion that offer, perhaps, more all-embracing clues to the meaning of the whole world process than the theoretical, explanatory aspects characteristic of metaphysical theism.

I have already adverted to these more central aspects in referring to love, wonder, and joy. What I have in mind, too, are the dimensions of spirituality and the sacred, which are found, as the phenomenologists and the historians of religion show us, throughout history and all over the globe. Both the mystical, giving expression to a sense of unity with the divine, and the numinous, giving expression to a sense of the awesome otherness of the divine, are pervasive features of human experience in the world of religion, in both its subjective and its objective senses. Again I stress the objective sense. I am interested in *what* is experienced: dimensions, modalities of the real, which themselves call for metaphysical explanation. What does it tell us about the cosmos that it evolves mystics and opens itself up to mystical penetration and becomes the vehicle of the sacred?

Religion has its dark side, of course. The problem of evil is found as much here as elsewhere. But so is the problem of good. What does it tell us about the cosmos that it evolves saints (and the communion of saints) in every developed culture and in every developed religion?

I can do no more than touch on these issues at the close of this chapter. The limitations of such holistic metaphysical thinking are obvious and great. In particular, the huge variety of world-views and world philosophies, not least those stemming from the world religions, contrast most strikingly with the relative uniformity of the scientific world-view. Yet, how much this uniform scientific *Weltanschauung* leaves out of account! For all its diversity, and I have drawn attention also to its commonalities, the kind of metaphysical thinking that attends seriously to the heights and depths of mind, freedom, morality, art, philosophy, and religion certainly encourages us to accept as plausible the view that it is theism that offers the best explanation of a world productive of these things.

2

The Rationality of Revelation

THE CASE sketched in the last chapter for supposing theistic metaphysics to offer the best explanation of a world productive of mind, freedom, morality, art, philosophy, and religion was an example of what, traditionally, has been called 'natural theology'. It has often been remarked that such a case proceeds by assembling a whole range of considerations which only when taken together can be seen to constitute a plausible case.

The logic of such cumulative case arguments has been explored and commended by such writers as Joseph Butler in *The Analogy of Religion*,[1] John Henry Newman in *A Grammar of Assent*,[2] F. R. Tennant in *Philosophical Theology*,[3] and, in recent philosophy of religion, Basil Mitchell in *The Justification of Religious Belief*[4] and Richard Swinburne in *The Existence of God*.[5] This, more recent work has been interestingly discussed by Robert Prevost in *Probability and Theistic Explanation*[6] (where preference is expressed for Mitchell's informal approach over Swinburne's use of formal logic) and by William J. Abraham in his contribution to the Mitchell *Festschrift*.[7] Most of this recent work—and the same is true of Tennant—has concerned itself with cumulative case arguments in natural theology: that is, with the case for a theistic world-view, although, as Abraham notes, Mitchell, like Butler and Newman before him, does extend the argument to include the case for taking revelation seriously as well. It is this extension of cumulative case arguments to include appeals to revelation that is going to provide the subject-matter of the rest of this book.

In this chapter I propose to examine the relation between natural theology and revealed theology and to defend the rationality of including appeals to revelation in a cumulative case for Christian belief. I shall argue that such appeals consist partly in appeals to history understood as the vehicle of divine revelation and partly in appeals to the inner logic and power of Christian doctrine. I shall also argue that, if Christian apologetics includes, not only a case for a theistic metaphysics as the best explanation of the world in which we find ourselves, but also a case for seeing history and particular strands in history as the vehicles of divine revelation, then really there is no sharp distinction to be drawn between natural and revealed theology. Apologetics includes both. (Please note that the phrase 'revealed theology' is shorthand for a theology which appeals to revelation. No one is suggesting that any theology as such is revealed!)

I hold natural theology to consist, first, in setting out a case for taking theism to offer the best explanation of a contingent world capable of evolving life, mind, personality, community, culture, and religion, and, secondly, in critical reflection on what such a theistic metaphysics must involve. I take revealed theology to consist, first, in setting out a case for taking some specific historical phenomenon, be it a series of events, a book, or a life story, as specially revelatory of the divine, and, secondly, in critical reflection on the illuminating and explanatory power of such an allegedly revelation-based theology for our understanding, not only of the world as it is, but also of the human predicament, its resolution, and our destiny.

The main difference between natural theology and revealed theology, on this view, is that the former appeals to facts about the world and human life that are available at any place and any time, while the latter appeals to facts that become available only through specific strands in world history. Of course, particular historical developments, such as the rise of modern science, do affect natural theology quite considerably, positively as well as negatively; and particular revelation-claims do become generally open to critical scrutiny in the course of history. But revelation-claims tend to remain embedded in specific religious traditions and communities, whereas scientific knowledge rapidly transcends its historical roots. So, while natural theologies are, as it were, the common products of world religion and world philosophy, revealed theologies are the products of specific faith traditions, Jewish, Christian, Muslim, Hindu, and so on. The point I wish to stress here is that both appeals, the appeal to nature and the appeal to revelation, are rational appeals. It is in this sense that revealed theology is being assimilated to natural theology. Both play their part in apologetic, in the cumulative case—the case, that is, not just for theism, but for Christian theism (or, indeed, for any other world religion's theism).

In philosophical theology we do not rest our case on any appeal to authority. We argue the case both for theism and, in the present case, for Christian doctrine. We should not, of course, dismiss appeals to authority *tout court*. They have a place in all disciplines, not least those of natural science. It is not possible to go back to square one and argue everything from scratch all the time. Acknowledged authorities yield short cuts in argument. Where they are not acknowledged, one either *does* have to argue the case oneself, or else one has to make a rational case for trusting the authority in question. As is well known, Thomas Aquinas did not, and could not, in his *Summa Contra Gentiles*, cite Scripture as an authority. The Christian Scriptures were not an acknowledged authority for the 'Gentiles'. But even in his *Summa Theologiae*, where the Scriptures (and also the Fathers and Aristotle, 'the philosopher') are cited as authorities in the paragraphs *sed contra*, those paragraphs do not carry the weight of the argument. The doctrine is defended rationally in the *responsio* paragraphs and in the replies to objections. Admittedly, Thomas did regard the articles of faith, such as the doctrines of the Incarnation and the Trinity, as something given, not themselves capable of independent demonstration (unlike the existence of God and God's basic attributes).[8] Thomas himself did not assimilate revealed theology to natural theology. All the same, the rational exploration and defence of Christian doctrine which Thomas undertook can be seen to play a part in specifically Christian apologetic. As Austin Farrer put it, à propos of the doctrine of the Incarnation: 'the longer I go on trying to tell you about this, the more I become convinced that the job that really wants doing is to expound the formula rather than to justify it; or, anyhow, that the justification required is identical with exposition.'[9]

It follows that Christian apologetic, where revealed theology is concerned, consists not only in appeal to certain historical factors: the story of Jesus, the response to his Resurrection, the emergence of the Church and its Scriptures, but also in the rational exposition and justification of the Christian doctrines themselves. But a similar point can be made about natural theology. This too consists not only in appeal to the factors considered in Chapter 1—that is to say, in a posteriori appeal to certain key elements in the world—but also in a priori reasoning about the necessities involved. This occurs most notably, of course, in the Ontological Argument, which attempts to prove God's necessary being, but we find it also, more generally, in explorations of the logic of theism, showing what must be true of the infinite, absolute, creator God. I know that the latter type of reasoning has been dubbed 'rational theology', by F. R. Tennant, for example,[10] and contrasted with natural theology. But there is a case for using the phrase 'rational theology' as an umbrella term for all the forms of Christian apologetic under scrutiny here, for both a posteriori and a priori reasoning in connection with both natural and revealed theology.

It will be clear that I am not restricting the a priori element of philosophical theology to the sphere of *fides quaerens intellectum*, faith seeking understanding. Certainly Christian apologetic is an activity by Christian thinkers from within the faith community of the Christian Church. A non-Christian may well be interested in, and capable of, exploring the rationality of Christian belief; but he or she is unlikely to be commending it or arguing its case, although one hopes that the sympathetic unbeliever will wish to join in rebutting travesties or caricatures. But even the apologist, in defending and commending Christianity, does not necessarily presuppose faith. As in all serious dialogue, the apologist endeavours to put himself or herself in the unbeliever's shoes and, using the shared techniques of critical rationality (on which much more will have to be said), to build up a cumulative case for Christianity.

Such a cumulative case will, as I say, include elements of a priori reasoning. Consider the example of Anselm. The fact that Anselm's *Proslogion* is written in the form of a prayer addressed to God[11] has misled many recent commentators, notably Karl Barth,[12] into thinking that his so-called Ontological Argument is a purely internal piece of *fides quaerens intellectum*, designed to help his fellow monks, already committed to the faith, in respect of their self-understanding. But this is quite wrong. What Anselm thanks God for is enabling him to hit on an a priori argument which, he claims, refutes the fool who says there is no God. And certainly what interests us is the validity or invalidity of the argument. As Alvin Plantinga[13] and Keith Ward[14] have shown, this argument can still play a role in theistic apologetic. Anselm's willingness to suspend the actual context of Christian faith is even clearer when we turn to what would normally be thought of as revealed theology: namely, incarnation and atonement. In *Cur Deus Homo?*,[15] Anselm gives us a dialogue in which his interlocutor is provided with a rational argument to counter the infidel's ridicule about the Incarnation. He even assays a proof, *remoto Christo*, setting aside his actual Christology, of why it was necessary for God to become man in order to effect atonement. We may not think much of the argument. My point is simply that we cannot treat Anselm's rational apologetic as wholly internal to Christian faith, when he explicitly brackets off his actual faith position.

These a priori arguments, whether in natural theology or in revealed theology, will certainly contribute to the cumulative case for Christian belief. Appeal to the inner rationale of Christian doctrine will be the subject of our explorations in Chapter 5. But the larger part of the remainder of this book, that is, Chapters 3, 4, and 6, will be devoted to a posteriori arguments for Christian belief, and, in particular, to appeals to history.

But first I want to pursue this matter of the assimilation of revealed theology to natural theology, at least in respect of their common rationality. The work of Joseph Butler, H. H. Farmer, and James Barr will illustrate the possibility and fruitfulness of this assimilation.

Joseph Butler's *The Analogy of Religion Natural and Revealed to the Constitution and Course of Nature,* to give it its full title, has two parts: 'Of Natural Religion' and 'Of Revealed Religion'. Butler's method is the same in both, to show that arguments for theism, for the moral government of the world, for a future life beyond death, and for what he calls 'the particular system of Christianity' are all analogous to arguments concerning worldly matters, in respect of their cumulative effect and their overall probability, despite doubts. 'Probability is the very guide of life,' as Butler says in his introduction. I shall say more about probability in Chapter 4. The point I want to stress here is Butler's demonstration that cumulative, probabilistic, reasoning is just as effective where revelation is concerned as it is in natural theology. Reason, Butler observes, 'is indeed the only faculty we have wherewith to judge concerning anything, even revelation itself'.[16] And later he describes the kind of reasoning he has in mind. 'The evidence of Christianity', he says,

will be a long series of things, reaching, as it seems, from the beginning of the world to the present time, of great variety and compass, taking in both the direct, and the collateral proofs; and making up, all of them together, one argument: the conviction arising from which kind of proof may be compared to what they call the effect in architecture or other works of art; a result from a great number of things so and so disposed, and taken into one view.[17]

This is, of course, a classic example of a cumulative case argument.

The Rationality of Revelation

Before leaving Bishop Butler, I should like to dwell on two aspects of his treatment of revealed religion which will be important for our own concerns in this book. In Part II, Chapter 6, Butler deals with the objection from 'the Want of Universality in Revelation'. He has already argued for the importance of Christianity *vis-à-vis* both morality and salvation, and for the authority and dominion of Christ. But now he attempts to rebut the charge of unfairness arising from the particularity of revelation. Butler's reply takes the form characteristic of his whole approach in *The Analogy*: namely, of showing that all God's gifts are unequally distributed, natural as well as revealed, and that there is nothing unjust in this, if everyone will be judged according to their use of opportunities provided. He then goes on to supplement his argument for the importance of Christianity by developing what he called in the passage quoted earlier the 'direct' and 'collateral' proofs of Christianity.

The direct proofs, for Butler, are the traditional, and quintessentially eighteenth-century, appeals to miracle and prophecy. These appeals, even when made in Butler's characteristically careful, probabilistic manner, are unlikely to be thought decisive in our post-critical age. We have learned to be suspicious of miracle, on theological as well as critical-historical grounds, and tend to prefer an account of divine action in terms of mediated providence (I return to this point in Chapter 4). All the same, appeal to the Resurrection of Jesus Christ still plays a central role in Christian apologetic, and my treatment of this important factor in the justification of Christian belief in Chapter 4 will be very much in the spirit of Butler's argument here.

The appeal to prophecy and fulfilment is already being handled with some sophistication by Butler himself, and our modern understanding both of typology and of prophetic insight (rather than straight prediction) will reinforce an attitude of some reserve about such appeals. All the same, the penetration and power of prophetic religion, scriptural and post-scriptural, are still going to play a part in the justification of Christian belief.

Of particular interest to us is Butler's treatment of the 'collateral' proofs, or 'circumstantial evidences', as he now calls them, in the construction of a single cumulative argument. For his appeal here is to historical revelation: the doctrines and precepts of Christianity, he says, are historical facts which reason could not have discovered beforehand, but which reason can now assess for their weight and significance. And taking all the evidence together, he modestly concludes that 'the general scheme of Christianity, and the principle parts of it, are conformable to the experienced constitution of things, and the whole perfectly credible'.[18] My own treatment of historical revelation in the rest of this book will again be very much in the spirit of Butler's argument here. But the principal point I take from Butler at this stage is that the appeal to nature and the appeal to historical revelation are elements in a single, rational, cumulative apologetic argument for Christian belief.

I next consider the views of H. H. Farmer, as we find them especially in the first chapter of his Gifford Lectures, *Revelation and Religion*, a chapter entitled 'Natural Theology and Christian Philosophy'.[19] After surveying a number of different understandings of the phrase 'natural theology', Farmer proposes to accept Bacon's definition: namely, 'the knowledge of God which may be had by the light of nature and the consideration of created things'.[20] He then observes that the reasonings of natural theology 'always draw some of their power . . . from the fact that something of natural religion . . . is concomitantly active' in the mind of one's interlocutor. This is debatable. The point has something of an air of hedging one's bets about it. I dare say that arguments for theism will only fully convince if they find confirmation in a person's experience; but it ought to be possible to reflect critically on the arguments themselves without any prior commitment. To start with, they can surely be examined hypothetically.

Farmer's next point is more persuasive. He remarks that any formulation of a unifying comprehensive world-view will involve not only examination of the empirical data provided by the world—namely, its existence and its actual nature—but also an element of constructive imagination arising from certain prior insights and convictions. This is fair comment, provided that those insights and convictions are themselves examined critically in respect of their power to make sense of the data.

But the point of greatest interest for our present purposes is the way in which Farmer goes on to suggest that a distinctively Christian theism might be advanced, to start with, hypothetically—Farmer himself now puts it like that—as a coherent world-view making most sense of all the data. By a distinctively Christian theism, Farmer says, he means a theism of incarnation and reconciliation. For the central affirmation of Christian theism is the affirmation that 'God has made unique, final and saving revelation of Himself as personal in history through Jesus Christ'.[21] Farmer even goes so far as to suggest that an attempt to construct such a Christian world-view can be brought under the rubric of natural theology, provided 'nothing is introduced in a merely authoritarian and overriding way and regarded as outside the scope of critical examination'.[22]

Without wishing to endorse this extension of the scope of natural theology, I think we can claim Farmer as an ally in the cause of bridging the gap between natural theology and revealed theology in so far as he is undoubtedly assimilating the latter to the former in respect of willingness to submit Christian appeals to historical revelation to critical scrutiny for their power to form a more comprehensive and, as we might put it, more existentially convincing world-view.

Farmer concludes his opening chapter by outlining the project for the rest of his book: namely, the provision of a distinctively Christian theology or philosophy of religion—that is to say, of the fact and history of religion in the life of mankind. Clearly, an integral part of the rational case for specifically Christian theism will be the sense it can make of the whole history of religions. This will form the topic of my own Chapter 3, and I shall be returning to Farmer's book in the course of my investigations there.

The third name mentioned above was that of James Barr. Here I have in mind his Gifford Lectures, *Biblical Faith and Natural Theology*[23] and Chapter 27 of his *The Concept of Biblical Theology*,[24] the chapter entitled 'Natural Theology within Biblical Theology'. Barr shows how much in the Old and New Testaments comes pretty close to natural theology, not only the often cited texts from Paul's speech on the Areopagus and Romans 1 and 2, but also the creation narratives, the Wisdom literature, the Bible's legal and moral teaching ('After all, the legal principles of non-Israelite peoples did not generally enjoin murder, theft and adultery as desirable practices,' as Barr rather nicely puts it), and, not least, the parables of Jesus, which explicitly draw on nature and 'publicly available knowledge'. It is in this connection that Barr observes that 'the distinction between revealed and natural theology is overcome'.[25] He even cites Karl Barth, from *Church Dogmatics*, iv. 3, on the parables being what Barth calls 'the prototype of the order in which there can be other true words alongside the one word of God'; and he could have gone on to refer to the remarkable way in which Barth speaks there of 'other lights' and 'parables of the Kingdom' in which God raises up witnesses to the one Word. Admittedly Barth takes back with the other hand what he has given with one hand by saying that only in the light of the one Word are these other words recognizable, but Barr could well accuse the arch opponent of natural theology of special pleading here.

Barr cites a number of authors—Claus Westermann, Gerald Downing, Dietrich Ritschl, Hendrikus Berkhof, and even William J. Abraham—as questioning any simplistic or exclusive use of the term 'revelation'. Barr himself inclines toward forswearing its use altogether. In writing of the way in which the natural theology of the Bible needs to be modified in the light of modern ecological concerns, he says that critical involvement in this task 'would necessarily include the integration of this natural theology with the central theological themes which used to be called "special revelation" '.[26] This may be going too far. Neither Berkhof nor Abraham would wish to drop the term 'revelation'. But they do question its exclusive use in Christocentric theology, not least its restriction to the view that special revelation occurred only in the past. My own retention of the phrase 'revealed theology' will be more in line with this non-exclusive use. Barr's concluding remark, however, that 'the Bible itself points to things that come from outside and—at least sometimes—welcomes these resources',[27] is entirely compatible with Berkhof's and Abraham's non-exclusive use of the term 'revelation'.

To sum up the main point being made here with reference to the contributions of Butler, Farmer, and Barr: Christian apologetic consists in a cumulative set of appeals, first to general features of the world and of human experience, and then to particular strands in world history, strands which, it is claimed, throw light on everything, including what is wrong with the world. These historical strands, comprising both events and their interpretations and culminating in a very specific historical strand, are held to disclose and provide the necessary resources for the world's and our transformation and renewal. They are also held, up to a point, to lift the veil on the ultimate goal of the whole world process. All these data, from both nature and history, are subject to critical scrutiny and evaluation for their capacity to come up with a total world-view, providing, among other things, the best theory of everything. That theory includes, as I say, the best explanation of the world's existence and of the way the world is, the best way of individual and social liberation, and the best prognosis for the future of creation. The appeals to history, which I shall be examining in Chapters 3, 4, and 6, are an integral part of this cumulative case.

To the extent that such a cumulative case includes appeals to key factors of both nature and history, it certainly exemplifies an evidentialist approach. This is clear from my emphasis on appeals to history as evidence in support of Christian theism. But the cumulative case includes much else besides. As already noted, it includes elements of a priori reasoning, spelling out the necessities involved in a theistic world-view; it also includes negative apologetic, rebutting objections to Christian theism; and, as was clear from both Butler and Farmer, it includes explication of what one might call the inner rationale of Christian theism. In other words, it includes spelling out the sense and power of developed Christian doctrine. This aspect of the cumulative case will be explored in Chapter 5.

While all these factors, taken together, do constitute an argument in support of Christian belief, I must persist in denying the charge of pursuing a foundationalist approach. This will become clear if we compare and contrast what I am trying to do here with what has been dubbed by Terence Penelhum[28] 'the Basic Belief Apologetic', associated most notably with Alvin Plantinga. Plantinga's opposition to foundationalism, and, for that matter, to evidentialism, in religious epistemology is well known. For Plantinga, belief in God and the central credal beliefs of Christianity are not held on the basis of other beliefs or because of any evidence cited in their favour. They are basic beliefs structuring the Christian's whole worldview and practice. Moreover, he insists quite specifically that such basic beliefs are not held because they explain anything.[29] They are warranted, according to Plantinga, if they are true, solely because they are the products of properly functioning faculties, designed by God with the purpose of yielding truth. Where theistic beliefs are concerned, those faculties include the *sensus divinitatis*—that is, an inner feeling for divinity, in-built by our Creator. Where the specifically Christian beliefs are concerned, these are, ultimately speaking, the product of the internal operation of the Holy Spirit, not bypassing our God-given faculties, however, but healing them and working through them.

There is nothing irrational about this so-called Reformed epistemology. Indeed, this theory of warrant spells out, according to Plantinga, the rationality of Christian belief. It shows how faith is, in fact, a form of knowledge; for warrant is what turns true belief into knowledge. Moreover, as Penelhum says, this is a species of apologetic. Plantinga is *defending* the rationality of Christian belief. He is also past master at negative apologetic, as is shown by his work on the free-will defence *vis-à-vis* the problem of evil and by his sustained rebuttals of alleged defeaters of, or objections to, theism in general and Christian belief in particular. And against those who argue that a Basic Belief Apologetic could be used to justify any belief system, however crazy, Plantinga argues powerfully that such crazy systems, unlike Christian theism, can be shown to have false premisses.[30]

All the same, it might well be suggested that Plantinga's religious epistemology is the direct opposite of what is being advocated here. Where I am urging the assimilation of revealed theology to natural theology in respect of their common rational scrutability, is not Plantinga repudiating natural theology altogether? Where I am proposing an appeal to an accumulation of evidence in support of both theism and Christian doctrine, and indeed inviting their consideration hypothetically as yielding the best explanation of all the data, is not Plantinga repudiating the need for any such support? Where I have explicitly distanced my apologetic strategy from the purely internalist task of faith seeking understanding, is not Plantinga simply presupposing faith?

However, I do not think that the two positions are quite so polarized as might appear. It would be perfectly possible to adopt Plantinga's basic belief stance, regard it hypothetically, and then look not for some inappropriate external foundation, but for a number of supporting or buttressing arguments, both in debate with unbelief and in response to doubt. Plantinga admits that, on his view, Christian belief is warranted if true, but he remains curiously coy about the defence of its truth, apart from negative apologetic refuting objections. I have allowed an important role for negative apologetic. But why stop there?

In fact, it turns out that Plantinga himself is not, after all, implacably opposed to positive apologetic. In sections of his article, 'Christian Philosophy at the End of the 20th Century',[31] he commends positive apologetic, not least the work of Swinburne; lists a whole host of good theistic arguments that cry out for articulation; and praises the work done by Christian philosophers in philosophical theology, deepening our grasp and understanding of the central doctrines of the Christian faith. All that Plantinga's basic belief epistemology requires is repudiation of the view that, without such arguments, Christian belief would be unjustified or unwarranted.

It can certainly be agreed that the rationality of Christian faith does not consist in the accumulation of supporting arguments and evidence. As pointed out at the beginning of Chapter 1, few people are actually argued into faith that way. I acknowledged there that most religious believers affirm their basic beliefs as an aspect of their participation in convictional communities, to use McClendon and Smith's phrase again,[32] in which they have been brought up or to which they have been converted.

It can also be agreed that for many, if not most, believers, an appeal to experience plays a more central role than an appeal to supporting arguments. The epistemological force of appeal to one's own religious experience has been expertly analysed by William Alston in his book *Perceiving God*;[33] although it is important to realize that not all religious experience is of the striking, *sui generis* kind illustrated and explored by Alston. For many believers, religious experience is more a matter of the sense of being forgiven, strengthened, called, or graced with peace, joy, wonder, and the love of one's fellow creatures, all these experiential states being aspects of their participation in the convictional communities of Christianity.

But even if the rationality and warrant of Christian belief do not consist in the accumulation of supporting arguments, the question still arises as to how far, if at all, its credibility requires or depends on such support. After all, a Christian basic belief structure of the type analysed by Plantinga has a certain vulnerability in a world where there are many unbelievers and many members of other, non-crazy, convictional communities with comparable basic beliefs. Admittedly, if true, the Christian faith does have unshakeable foundations in the activity of God, and cannot be said to depend on anything else. But any Christian individual's conviction of its truth can collapse. People do lose their faith. Even Plantinga allows the need for the rebuttal of alleged defeaters. But the need for positive support, both in the interests of meeting doubt and in the interests of apologetic, is equally pressing.

But, to repeat, does the credibility of Christian belief *depend* on such support? Against Plantinga, it could be argued that a basic belief structure, however sure its foundation in the activity of God, if true, can still collapse if it lacks the support of buttressing arguments. Not that every Christian has to be able to produce the arguments. The warrant, and thus the rationality, of someone's basic beliefs do not depend on his or her ability to come up with a successful cumulative case for Christian theism. But if no one could do it, the credibility and the future of Christianity—humanly speaking, at least—would be in doubt.

The Rationality of Revelation

Of course, the credibility of Christianity does not stand or fall by each and every one of the elements in the best-constructed cumulative case that may be advanced in its support. Restricting ourselves to the evidentialist elements in the cumulative case, let us consider how indispensable appeals to nature and appeals to history are for the kind of apologetic envisaged here. Take, for example, some of the elements in a characteristic modern design argument for the existence of God. The basic fact being appealed to here is, as I stressed in Chapter 1, the capacity of the world stuff, the fundamental energy quanta and forces, operating under the fundamental laws of nature, to come up with the conditions of life and with living, conscious, rational, personal beings, and with all the products of their cultures. This basic fact is clearly a truth condition, a *sine qua non*, of our being here and considering these questions, let alone of any theistic or Christian belief. But it is more than a truth condition. When considered in connection with the values of goodness, beauty, and truth, and their embodiment in the cultures and religions that have appeared over the course of evolution, we find positive pointers towards some form of theism as their best explanation. Some such combination of teleological and axiological arguments is surely indispensable in any supporting apologetic.

Other elements in this stage of the cumulative case are by no means indispensable. Consider, for example, arguments based on the so-called anthropic principle. It looks as if conditions in the early stages of cosmic expansion subsequent to the Big Bang had to be finely tuned in a whole number of remarkable ways if ever the conditions for life and, *a fortiori*, intelligent life were to be realized. Appeal to the fine-tuning of the universe finds its place in design arguments such as those of Richard

Swinburne;[34] and many, including myself, find them highly persuasive. But, as the Astronomer Royal has shown,[35] there are alternative explanations, albeit involving very extravagant postulation of multiple—indeed innumerable—'universes', so that ours just happens to be one where the factors coincided fruitfully. Clearly, appeal to fine-tuning is not indispensable. The plausibility of theism does not depend on Swinburne, rather than Rees, being right about this.

Natural theology, then, includes both indispensable and dispensable appeals. Note too how natural theology, with its case for theism based on general features of the world, shades into the realm of appeals to history, to the emergence and development of values and their embodiment, not least in the history of religions, to which we shall be turning in the next chapter.

But when we move on to revealed theology, and in particular to very specific strands and events in history, construed as revelatory, we find ourselves, without doubt, in the realm of indispensable appeals. For Christianity is unintelligible without appeal to the story of Jesus—his life, teaching, passion, death, and Resurrection. All that, too, is unintelligible without its background and context in the faith of Israel. Again, the faith of Israel being what it was and is, and the story of Jesus being what it was, are not simply truth conditions of Christianity. It is not just that the Christian faith would be falsified if it were proved that Jesus never existed or that he was a murderer or a rapist, or indeed that he was never crucified, or that the Resurrection did not happen. Rather, it is the positive facts of his life, teaching, and fate and their aftermath that constitute the principal evidence for the truth of Christianity. As we shall see in Chapter 4, these facts are not *merely* historical facts, but they include historical facts; and it is the history that provides the indispensable evidence.

Of course, in speaking of the events that gave rise to the doctrines of the Incarnation and the Resurrection, we are speaking not simply of what supports Christian belief, but of what constitutes it. These are among the foundations of Christianity. But this is not to go back to foundationalism in epistemology. These are the ontological foundations of Christianity, if it is true. As Plantinga recognizes, the basic beliefs and the basic belief structure of Christianity are, if true, founded, ontologically, upon the activity of God. Their warrant does not consist in appeal to other more basic beliefs. But Plantinga, curiously, does not explore the implications of the fact that the activity of God that grounds Christianity, if true, includes not only the internal operation of the Holy Spirit, but God's actions in creation and providence, culminating in the Incarnation, the Resurrection, and their after-effects. Plantinga refers to creation, sin, incarnation, atonement, resurrection, and eternal life as the main lines of Scripture's teaching,[36] comprising the basic beliefs whose warrant he has analysed in terms of God's inspiration of our faculties when properly functioning as we read the Scriptures. What he does not give sufficient attention to is the indispensable support for these basic beliefs to be found in the historical evidence for God's action in history. Plantinga devotes many pages of negative apologetic to what many may deem a somewhat crude demolition of the historical-critical method's threat to the credibility of the main lines of Scripture's teaching; but he does not explore the possibilities of positive apologetic based on careful, critical sifting of the historical evidence.

In fact, the situation with appeals to history as an integral part of Christian apologetics is, as Butler saw, strictly analogous to appeals to nature as an integral part of Christian apologetic. However tentative, partial, or probabilistic these appeals may be, they contribute to the cumulative case for recognition of God's action in creation and providence, and they offer positive support for the belief system of the Christian religion. There being some such support is surely indispensable if the basic beliefs of Christianity, humanly speaking at least, are to be sustained.

Appeals to experience, too, are surely indispensable. If the case for Christian theism failed to find confirmation in believers' experience, in the manner analysed by Alston in his aforementioned book and summarized in a previous paragraph, the cumulative case would not convince.

To return to Plantinga's contribution: in an interesting review article on Plantinga's *Warranted Christian Belief* and Bruce Marshall's *Trinity and Truth*, entitled 'Philosophy of Religion or Philosophical Theology?',[37] Andrew Moore criticizes Plantinga for being more of a philosopher of religion than a philosophical theologian. But I am not persuaded by the way in which Moore makes this distinction. For Moore, in philosophy of religion, 'theological positions tend to be subsumed within a broader philosophical framework', whereas in philosophical theology, philosophy, though used as a tool, is in the end 'subservient to theology'. 'Crudely and briefly put', writes Moore, 'a philosophical theologian bows to revelation, a philosopher of religion to reason'.[38] No follower of Bishop Butler could possibly accept that last formulation. I have already quoted from Butler: 'Reason is indeed the only faculty we have wherewith to judge concerning anything, even revelation itself.' Reason is the common and essential tool of philosophers and theologians alike. There are indeed some philosophies that do subsume theology within a broader philosophy—the philosophies of Kant, Hegel, and Whitehead, to name but three. But philosophical analysis in its Anglo-Saxon and even Wittgensteinian forms is not committed to such subsumption. And certainly Plantinga uses philosophy not as a controlling system, but as an analytical tool for articulating, clarifying, and defending a robustly Christian world-view. He is a Christian philosopher, and has famously advised Christian philosophers to show confidence in their Christian convictions, and to use their rational, philosophical skills in exploring the problems of both theology and philosophy from a Christian point of view.

Moore attempts to contrast Plantinga with Donald MacKinnon, who, says Moore, should be regarded as a philosophical theologian rather than a philosopher of religion, precisely because he was aware of the fact that 'philosophy, whether metaphysics, descriptive or speculative, or logic, is never master in theology but its indispensable servant'.[39] But MacKinnon was a philosopher, not because he fitted the stereotype of a philosopher through his celebrated eccentricities, as Moore suggests, but because of his training and skill in that subject. It was his penetrating philosophical acumen that enabled him to appreciate rationally the inappropriateness of making theology subservient to philosophy. And the same is true of Plantinga.

Of course, philosophers applying their analytic skills to theological topics have to become theologically literate, and MacKinnon might well be thought to be more theologically literate than Plantinga. But this does not entail the subjection of philosophy to theology, still less of reason to revelation.

Philosophy of religion and philosophical theology are better differentiated by reference to their respective subject-matters, although, as we have already seen, they tend to shade into one another and overlap quite extensively. In the philosophy of religion, philosophers, and theologians prepared to school themselves in philosophy, examine and reflect on religion in all its main forms, but in particular on theistic metaphysics and epistemology. In philosophical theology, philosophers and theologians turn their attention to what I called the inner rationale of doctrines and doctrinal systems developed on the basis, allegedly, of revelation, and to the way in which these factors contribute to the cumulative case for Christian belief, if that is the tradition under scrutiny. In this latter aspect, we see philosophical theology itself playing a role in the philosophy of religion. To mention some examples, Richard Swinburne has moved on from his earlier philosophy of religion trilogy, *The Coherence of Theism*,[40] *The Existence of God*,[41] and *Faith and Reason*,[42] to his series of books on philosophical theology, *Responsibility and Atonement*,[43] *Revelation*,[44] *The Christian God*,[45] and *Providence and the Problem of Evil*[46]—although with the last of these, admittedly, he reverts to the philosophy of religion. But throughout, he approaches all these matters as a philosopher and contributes the skills of philosophical analysis to the exploration of themes in both natural and revealed theology. The same was true of MacKinnon, whether he was writing on metaphysics, as he was in his Gifford Lectures,[47] or on the relation of the doctrines of the Incarnation and the Trinity.[48]

Plantinga, too, is very much a philosopher, albeit a self-proclaimed Christian philosopher. His main concerns fall within the sphere of the philosophy of religion: namely, the concept of God, epistemology, and negative apologetics; although his preoccupation with the epistemology of Christian belief and his defence of Christianity against alleged defeaters bring him closer to the concerns of philosophical theology. He has not himself devoted time and energy to the philosophical analysis of mainline Christian doctrines, in the manner of other Christian philosophers, such as Thomas V. Morris[49] and Peter van Inwagen,[50] whose work he presumably had in mind when praising such contributions in the aforementioned essay. This kind of work will be called upon in Chapter 5 to illustrate the way in which analysis and defence of Christian doctrine also forms an integral part of Christian apologetic.

Most work in the philosophy of religion, and much work in philosophical theology, is being done by philosophers rather than by theologians, often, of course, by Christian philosophers. In an ideal world, the practitioners of these disciplines would be equally at home and schooled in both philosophy and theology, as was the case in the thirteenth century with Thomas Aquinas and in the twentieth with Austin Farrer. But such paragons are rare. Plantinga is perhaps exaggerating when he opines 'that the best work in philosophical theology—in the English speaking world and over the last quarter century—has been done not by theologians but by philosophers'.[51] Be that as it may, what one looks for are dialogue and co-operation between theologically literate philosophers and philosophically literate theologians. Current tensions are to be regretted.

There remains a difference to be noted between the approach of the philosophers and that of the theologians to both natural and revealed theology. This sometimes evokes unfair criticism of philosophers by theologians. 'Philosophy of religion', says Andrew Moore, 'prefers to discuss a generic and abstract theism.'[52] This smacks of the old objection that the god of the philosophers has nothing to do with the God of Abraham,

Isaac, and Jacob. But, of course, there is no such thing as the god of the philosophers. As I have written elsewhere, all that philosophers of religion are doing is 'abstracting for analysis elements implicit', or, I should add, explicit, 'in the more theologically rounded notions'.[53] The notion of eternity, for example, requires analysis; but there is nothing abstract about the notion of the eternal God, Creator of the world.

Another of Moore's *gravamina* is against the idea of Christianity being accepted because it offers the best explanation of everything. Here he endorses Plantinga's view: 'It is very welcome', Moore says, 'to find a philosopher acknowledging . . . that Christian belief is not ordinarily accepted because it is an *explanation* of anything.'[54] But, as already urged, the fact that such explanation does not form the basis of faith in no way entails depreciation of the claim that Christian faith can find support from a cumulative case argument to the effect that Christianity provides the best explanation of the world's existence and nature, and of the state we find ourselves in. What theologians often fail to appreciate is the apologetic force of standing back from one's commitments, looking at all aspects of the Christian faith hypothetically, and reflecting philosophically on the supporting evidence, the inner rationale, and the explanatory power of the Christian world-view. And while this is obviously not the dominant or characteristic mode of theological enquiry, the fact remains that both faith seeking understanding and Christian apologetic benefit from such disengaged reflection. Theologians, therefore, as well as philosophers of religion, are well advised to include these modes of operation within their repertoire.

It is high time something was said about the kind of rationality involved in the critical scrutiny of all theology, natural and revealed, being urged here upon philosophers and theologians alike, in the linked enterprises of examining the inner rationale of the Christian faith and engaging in Christian apologetic. In particular, what kind of rationality is involved in the construction and assessment of a cumulative case for a Christian worldview which includes appeals to nature, logic, history, and doctrine as integral parts of Christian apologetic?

To ask this question is to be reminded of the title of Alasdair MacIntyre's book, *Whose Justice? Which Rationality?*.[55] With exemplary clarity, MacIntyre raises the question of incommensurability between different tradition-constituted modes of enquiry, and challenges the Enlightenment paradigm of a single universal critical and practical rationality, shared by all educated people, whatever their background. Yet MacIntyre himself goes on to suggest that some traditions succeed better than others in coping with failures and offering more constructive solutions to the problems of moral and political life. These criteria of relative success and failure are suggestive of a more universal rationality after all. Indeed, MacIntyre now holds that teleological explanations of the good 'will be true if and only if the universe itself is teleologically ordered, and the only type of teleologically ordered universe in which we have good reason to believe is a theistic universe'.[56]

MacIntyre's recent work is primarily in the sphere of moral philosophy, and his concerns primarily those of practical rationality. With religion in general, and with Christianity in particular, we are indeed concerned with practice, but with practice embedded in theory. And the critical rationality involved in assessing the success or failure of a cumulative case argument for Christianity will, as I say, be concerned not only with the best explanation of the way the world is, but also with the best way of individual and social liberation, and the best prognosis for the future of creation. What I called a more existentially convincing world-view will contain putative answers to all three of Kant's fundamental questions: What can I know? What ought I to do? What may I hope?[57] Kant says that all the interests of reason, speculative as well as practical, combine in these three questions, but he himself treats them separately and imposes far too rigid and narrow restrictions on the scope of the speculative.

The kind of critical rationality employed in philosophical theology includes the theoretical and the practical within the scope of judgement, the topic of Kant's Third *Critique*,[58] albeit in a much more all-embracing sense than Kant envisaged there. The role of judgement in assessing the case for a specific world-view was stressed already by Butler in the passage quoted earlier, where he spoke of 'a great number of things so and so disposed, and taken into one view'. This key aspect of rationality was also stressed by Newman in his well-known section on the illative sense,[59] 'sense' here being a cognitive, not just an affective, faculty, a power of judgement seen in the good lawyer or historian, as Mitchell shows. Keith Ward, in his *Rational Theology and the Creativity of God*, speaks of 'synoptic rationality', a creative and imaginative facility of judgement and discernment, evaluating all the world's most significant features and fitting them into an overall pattern.[60] Michael Langford, in *A Liberal Theology for the Twenty-First Century*, subtitled *A Passion for Reason*, develops this understanding of the scope of human reason for the critical evaluation of philosophical and religious world-views.[61] Such comprehensive judgement involves not only the logic of deduction and induction, but also the cognitive elements in feeling, imagination,

and intuition, the resulting discernments all being subject to critical reflection and debate.

Theologians will realize that, in holding that theistic metaphysics, history as revelation, and Christian doctrine can and should be discussed openly for purposes of self-understanding, mutual comprehension, and apologetic, I am siding with Wolfhart Pannenberg, when, against Bernard Lonergan's insistence on conversion as a pre-condition of theological insight, he pleads for theology 'to be discussed without reservations in the context of critical rationality'.[62] There is much to be learned from Lonergan's work on insight and theological method, just as there is from Thomas Torrance's book, *God and Rationality*.[63] But it is surely a mistake to regard the logic of theological rationality as something wholly internal to the perspective of faith. Torrance, and Barth too, are entirely persuasive in their insistence on theological rationality being responsive to the unique nature of theology's object. But the supposition that theological thinking has its own logic, only available within the relation of grace and faith, has the same effect as Lonergan's insistence on conversion. It makes theology, natural or revealed, undiscussable, immune to criticism, and unsusceptible of being pondered hypothetically. This makes no sense at all where natural theology is concerned; and the assimilation of revealed theology to natural theology, which has been the burden of this chapter, suggests that revealed theology too ought not to be protected in this way, but rather should remain open to consideration by all in the context of critical rationality.

3

The Appeal to History I:
The History of Religions

We now turn to the way in which appeals to history exemplify the extension of our cumulative case for Christian belief from appeals to nature to appeals to revelation. I consider first the appeal to the history of religions. I am not, in the first instance, examining religion on the human scene as anything other than a widespread set of historical phenomena. Whether or not some ordering, or progression, or comparative evaluation is called for is not yet in question. It is simply the pluriform fact of religion in human history all over the globe that is being held to contribute to the cumulative case for Christian belief.

An immediate rejoinder to this might well take the following, twofold form. First, it might be argued that appeals to the fact of religion in general belong only to the natural theology stage of the cumulative case, along with other axiological arguments from the values of morality, art, culture, and philosophy, seeking the best explanation for the capacity of the world stuff to evolve such remarkable phenomena, as argued in Chapter 1. Secondly, it might be argued that an appeal to the history of religions in this sense could at best contribute

to the cumulative case for a religious view of the world, not a specifically Christian one.

But, as was argued in Chapter 2, natural theology tends to shade into revealed theology, and general features of the world into historically specific ones. Teleological (or design) arguments involve not only the general capacity of the world stuff to evolve personal and interpersonal life, but its capacity to come up with human history in all its fascinating diversity and particularity. The axiological arguments I mentioned just now (arguments, that is, from value) appeal not just to moral and aesthetic values in general, but also to the specific ethical communities and cultures and art-forms that have emerged in the course of human history. Appeals to religion world-wide are appeals not just to the fact, but to the nature, of religion as it has developed into the different faith communities in world history.

It is perfectly true that every developed faith, not only Christianity, is rooted in the wider history of religions. Consequently, there will be parallels in the way in which appeals are made to the history of religions in cumulative cases for Jewish belief, Muslim belief, Hindu belief, Buddhist belief, and so on, to the way in which they are made in the cumulative case for Christian belief. At a later stage we will indeed have to consider, comparatively, how well these various faiths succeed in making sense of the whole history of religions. But our particular concern, at the moment, is with the support given, over and above natural theology, by the history of religions to the cumulative case for Christian belief. As I hope to show later in this chapter, Christian anthropology and Christian theology are rooted in the fact and history of religion on the human scene. Christianity, no more than any other faith, dropped into the human scene out of the blue. I quote Bishop Butler again: 'The evidence of Christianity will be a long series of things, reaching, as it seems, from the beginning of the world to the present time.'[1]

Let us then consider some of the principal elements or dimensions of religion that might be appealed to at this stage of the cumulative case. First, we may cite the fact and nature of religious *experience* in pretty well every human community at every period of human history. Now, as mentioned in the previous chapter, the epistemology of religious experience has been explored in depth and in detail by William Alston in his book, *Perceiving God.*[2] Alston's treatment of what he calls 'The Christian Mystical Perceptual Doxastic Practice' will be considered later. At this stage, I am concerned with Alston's defence of the cognitive force of all the major forms of religious experience. The chief feature of his analysis is the comparison between mystical perception and sense perception. The argument is akin to Butler's argument in *The Analogy.* The credentials of sense perception are shown to be no better than those of mystical perception as far as epistemic justification is concerned. In neither case can we get outside the practice in order to justify it. But this 'epistemic circularity' does not prevent us from relying on sense perception. Why should it disqualify mystical perception?

I think it something of a pity that Alston uses the word 'mystical' for religious experience in general. The phenomenology of religion, as practised by Ninian Smart, for example,[3] has taught us to distinguish between the *mystical* strand in world religion, highlighting unitive experiences of various kinds, and the *numinous* strand in world religion, highlighting the sense of the holy and of the otherness and transcendence of

the religious object. Nor should religious experience be confined to these heightened states, whether mystical or numinous. Again, as pointed out in the last chapter, the ways in which ordinary believers in all religious contexts feel themselves sustained, addressed, called, rebuked, forgiven, loved, must also be reckoned with in any argument from religious experience.

Two other features of Alston's analysis deserve comment. Unlike Swinburne, who, in his treatment of religious experience in his book, *The Existence of God*,[4] concentrates on the individual's sense of the divine (both mediated and unmediated), Alston brings out the setting of believers' experiential claims in socially established practices of various kinds. This involves the embeddedness of experience in traditions of belief and, of course, reinforces the point made above that we are appealing to history when we appeal to the fact and nature of religious experience world-wide. For socially established practices are historical phenomena. We shall return to this point when we come to the question of comparative evaluation.

The other feature of Alston's analysis, and here he is at one with Swinburne, is his spelling out of the way in which appeals to experience fit in with, and mutually reinforce, other elements in the cumulative case for an all-embracing religious world-view, such as that of Christianity. Other elements, those of natural theology and those of a developed doctrinal system, purport to offer the best explanation of the world and of human history, and, as I stressed in Chapter 2 and will again in Chapter 5, the best diagnosis of the human condition and the best prognosis of the ultimate future. But 'mystical perception', to revert to Alston's phrase, does not offer explanatory support for a set of beliefs, but rather direct perceptual support for a religious world-view. This is the sense in which a tentative cumulative case argument might find experiential confirmation in the manner analysed by Austin Farrer in the first three chapters of his *Faith and Speculation*.[5] All the same, as Alston notes, it can still be argued that the best explanation of the fact and nature of religious experience is offered by a particular belief system. The interplay and mutual support of experience and belief go both ways.

The second element, or dimension, of religion that might be appealed to is the moral dimension. This is hardly a separate dimension. Religious experience, even mystical experience, is, in nearly all its manifestations, bound up with moral perceptions and moral demands. Divorced from morality, mysticism (in the narrower sense which, against Alston's usage, I have commended) can become a dangerous phenomenon, as R. C. Zaehner insists in *Our Savage God*.[6] Other types of religious experience, numinous, devotional, vocational, penitential, the sense of gratitude, even the sense of wonder, are suffused with moral value. And the more we appreciate Alston's point about the reciprocity of experience and belief, the more we shall appreciate the ethical dimension in the history of religions: namely, the formation and development of faith communities committed to some vision of the highest good, both personal and social, and its consequent demands upon us.

That the moral argument for the existence of God, like the argument from religious experience, is not simply another element in natural theology, appealing to a universal feature of the natural world, but rather consisting in a further appeal to history, and indeed to the history of religions, can be illustrated by a number of examples. Thus A. E. Taylor, in his Gifford Lectures, *The Faith of a Moralist*,[7] having argued that morality points beyond itself to an eternal good, to God, to divine grace, and to immortality, goes on to insist that a natural theology which takes the moral life seriously 'must take account of the initiative of the divine'. This involves abandoning the prejudice 'that there is any real opposition in principle between "philosophical" or "natural" and "historical" or "revealed" theology, or between a philosophical and an institutional religion',[8] the very point emphasized and defended in Chapter 2 of this book. Taylor proceeds, in his second volume, to spell out what this entails in chapters on 'Reason and Revelation' and 'Religion and the Historical' in ways that do justice both to the historical relativity of each religion and to the distinctive claims of Christianity.

Austin Farrer, in a piece entitled, on reprinting, 'A Moral Argument for the Existence of God',[9] suggests that the claim of our neighbour, however unlovely, upon our regard is rendered most plausible by the Christian doctrines of creation and redemption, in terms of which that neighbour can be seen as a child of God, destined for eternity. There is much to discuss about the premiss of this argument and about the Christian world-view proposed as its best explanation. My sole comment here is that Farrer's argument can hardly be construed as a piece of natural theology. It appeals to a specific, historically formed tradition of theistic doctrine: namely, the Christian religion.

Turning to George Mavrodes's essay, 'Religion and the Queerness of Morality',[10] we might indeed appear to have reverted to an element in natural theology. For the gist of Mavrodes's argument is that moral obligation in what he calls a 'Russellian' world (the reference, of course, being to the philosophy of Bertrand Russell)—a world, that is, in which we are simply the products of accidental collocations of atoms—is a very odd and inexplicable phenomenon. Moral obligation, he avers, cannot plausibly be held to be no more than a device conducive to our own good. Even if it were, it would still remain no more than a superficial phenomenon *vis-à-vis* such things as matter and energy, which alone are deep in a Russellian world. Mavrodes contrasts this with Kant's recognition that there cannot, in any reasonable way, be a moral demand upon me, unless reality is committed to morality in some deep way. For Mavrodes this implies the view that 'things like mind and purpose must also be deeper in the real world than they would be in a Russellian world'.[11] This might well attract us to some religious view of the world, he says. So far, the argument seems pretty general; but, as Mavrodes allows, it is only a beginning, a sketch waiting to be filled in. And he ends his essay with some remarks on the way in which his own religion, Christianity, makes sense of this queer phenomenon, morality. Other religions could, of course, be called upon in comparable ways.

That the moral argument involves appeal to the history of religions is also clear from Elizabeth Anscombe's much discussed paper 'Modern Moral Philosophy'.[12] With studied irony, Anscombe suggests that the concepts of moral obligation and moral duty ought to be jettisoned, since they are survivals, or derivations from survivals, from an earlier conception of ethics: namely, divine command theory, which, she insists, has historical origins, not only in the Judaeo-Christian tradition (Christianity, she says, derived its ethical notions from the Torah) but also in Stoicism and, one could presumably add, in other theistic religions. Mavrodes too appeals to Plato in this connection. We shall consider how well this squares with his reference to mind and purpose deep down when we come to the question of comparative evaluation.

The Appeal to History I

A substantial and important treatment of the religious framework of ethics is to be found in Robert Merrihew Adams's *Finite and Infinite Goods.*[13] I will concentrate here on the final section, 'The Epistemology of Value'. Adams first makes the important point that a theistic framework for ethics, offering as it does the most intuitively satisfying and realistic account of the critical stance essential to ethical theory, does not commit us to the view that knowledge of the good depends on knowledge of God. People were well aware of the wetness and drinkableness of water long before they came to know that water consists of H_2O. Similarly, recognition of human goodness and of the common good is widespread among people of any faith or none. This does not prevent theological ethics from providing the best explanation of goodness—of all goodness, not just sanctity—as reflecting a transcendent Good. Adams next offers an account of evaluative doxastic practices very much along the lines of Alston's account of 'mystical' doxastic practices. (I should explain that a 'doxastic' practice is a practical method of belief formation.) Like Alston, Adams stresses the social formation and critique of such practices, in different historical contexts. Of particular interest here is the way in which he ascribes this formation, ultimately, to divine revelation, to general revelation, not simply in respect of what is accessible through the exercise of our natural faculties alone, but in respect of the universal or widespread operation of divine grace or illumination. He reserves the notion of special revelation for revelation that is tied to particular historic religious traditions. This, of course, is to extend the scope of general revelation beyond that of natural theology, and to restrict the appeal to history to the more developed traditions in the history of religions. I have myself tended to move the other way and extend the scope of special revelation to cover the whole field of religious and moral awareness, just because this is nearly always already embedded in particular social practices.

Enough has been said to indicate the way in which appeal to the moral dimension can feature in appeals to the history of religions as part of the cumulative case for Christian, as for any developed religious, belief. A third dimension is provided by appeals to beauty. It was pointed out in Chapter 1 how philosophers, from Plato to Hegel and beyond, have seen art as a window into the eternal. The religious significance of beauty has been brought out by Patrick Sherry in *Spirit and Beauty: An Introduction to Theological Aesthetics*,[14] with special reference to Simone Weil, for whom the experience of beauty was an experience of God, sometimes, as for unbelievers, of the implicit love of God. This goes for natural beauty and for art. Both nature and culture can be seen, and are perhaps best seen, as vehicles of revelation. Where the latter, culture, is concerned, we are again in the realm of appeals to history.

In Chapter 1, I referred to another axiological argument, the argument from truth. In my own words: 'Our deep-rooted conviction that truth is a matter of discovery and not invention is best accounted for on the supposition of an infinite Mind that makes things what they are and preserves them as what they are for us to discover.'[15] This argument is all the stronger when we incorporate into its premises the truths of mind as well as of matter. The argument's conclusion is, of course, spelled out in many world philosophies, especially in the many forms of theistic metaphysics that are to be found developed in, and beyond, the history of religions. So once again we note that an argument in natural theology gets fleshed out historically in traditions that can claim to be best understood as vehicles of special revelation.

I return now to the question of how important these appeals to the experiential, moral, aesthetic, and metaphysical dimensions of the history of religions are to the cumulative case for specifically Christian belief. Well, clearly, they do more than contribute to the background and context of Christianity. Certainly Christianity has to be understood in relation to its Jewish context and background, a topic to be considered in the next chapter. And much has been said, and needs to be said, about the relation of the developing faith of Israel to Near Eastern religions more generally. But Christian anthropology requires a more universal grounding in the religious propensities of humankind and in the whole history of religions. This factor has both past and present dimensions. The former is captured by Wolfhart Pannenberg when he writes that it is natural for Christian theology 'to regard the history of religion as a history of the manifestation of the unity of deity which God himself controls on the path to revelation'.[16] In the light of what I have said already about the different historical channels of divine special revelation, it is reasonable to go further than Pannenberg and to admit that many developed religions, at least the theistic religions, could make similar cases for construing the whole history of religions this way. We should admit, too, that the non-theistic religions may be regarded as channels of awareness of, and commerce with, the transcendent. Without this general, albeit diverse, recognition of the openness of humanity to the transcendent, no developed religion would be intelligible. With it, the case for taking putative revelation seriously is enhanced. But, as I say, this is a matter of present as well as past recognition. The anthropological point holds, not only for the origins of Christianity and of other developed faiths, but also for Christian belief today. Christian apologetic is helped, not hindered, by the presence world-wide of the experiential, moral, aesthetic, and metaphysical factors to which I have been attending in adverting to the history of religions.

Nevertheless, the diversity of religions does constitute a problem for the epistemology, and for the justification, of Christian belief. A cumulative case in support of Christian belief, or indeed in support of any other religious world-view, which moves beyond natural theology into revealed theology and appeals to both nature and history, in the way I have been adumbrating here, is bound to have to face up to the diversity of religious world-views that have emerged and been developed in the course of the history of religions. We cannot postpone any longer the question of the possibility, perhaps the necessity, of comparative evaluation. This is no easy task, especially nowadays, when greatly increased knowledge of the history of religions has combined with historically and philosophically induced scepticism about the very notions of universal history and of progress in history to render us highly suspicious of absolutist claims for Christianity.

Take Hegel, for example. For all the astonishing range of his *Lectures on the Philosophy of Religion*,[17] no student of comparative religion today could possibly endorse his placing of the religions of India in the category of nature religions, prior to the recognition of the Absolute as free subjectivity. The roles of Jewish religion and of Greek religion in precipitating this recognition are a fascinating theme in Hegel's history of philosophy; but his evident sympathy for the latter, Greek religion, leads him to do scant justice to the former, Judaism, which he accuses, along with Islam, of legalism and parochialism, incapable of overcoming the alienation between man and the Absolute, or of achieving genuine universality. As is well known, Hegel saw Christianity as the absolute religion, in so far as it realized, albeit only at the level of representation, both these factors: the overcoming of alienation through the idea of incarnation and universality (with some providential help from the Roman Empire) through its own progressive grasp of world history's self-understanding. It would be a bold student or philosopher of religion who could embrace all that today.

Schleiermacher's understanding of religion or piety as the felt awareness of being absolutely dependent[18] was less bound up with universal history or with progress in history than was Hegel's. Schleiermacher's typology, while allowing spiritual significance to all forms of religion, accords the priority to what he calls the highest level of God-consciousness: namely, the monotheistic forms of religious affection. It is a mark of the distance we have come from early modern liberal Protestantism that no one would concede today that this highest plane is confined to Judaism, Christianity, and Islam. Moreover, Schleiermacher's relegation of Judaism and Islam to lower levels than Christianity, the former because of its restriction to a particular people, the latter because of its subordination of the teleological to the aesthetic—that is, the active to the passive—is bound to strike present-day readers as highly implausible. However, Schleiermacher's characterization of the essence of Christianity as consisting in the fact that in it everything is related to the redemption accomplished by Jesus of Nazareth cannot be so easily dismissed; and I shall be returning to this key factor in the next chapter.

The Appeal to History I

With Ernst Troeltsch we come to a historian of religion and a theologian much closer to contemporary sensibility. It is fascinating to observe how Troeltsch moved from a guarded affirmation of the absoluteness of Christianity in 1901 to a conviction of the historical relativity and equal validity of the great world faiths in 1923. In *The Absoluteness of Christianity* (1901),[19] Troeltsch was still prepared to place religions primarily of law, such as Judaism and Islam, on a lower plane than religions of redemption, such as Christianity and the Indian religions. Even in this early book, a certain ambivalence appears at this point. On the one hand, Troeltsch says, 'It is necessary to make a *choice* between redemption through meditation on transcendent Being or non-Being and redemption through faithful trusting participation in the person-like character of God, the ground of all life and of all genuine value.'[20] On the other hand, he claims that historical study of religions shows that Christianity synthesizes a greater range of developmental tendencies in the history of religions than any other religion. Even so, Christianity points to an Absolute beyond history. Its own personal theism is accorded only a relative superiority, and Troeltsch is critical of the way it has tended to absolutize either Jesus or the Church.

By the time he wrote 'The Place of Christianity among the World Religions' (1923),[21] Troeltsch had come round to embracing a much more consistent relativism. He now suggests that Christian conviction of the truth of Christianity has final and unconditional validity only for those formed by its historically and culturally mediated value system and spirituality. Others, formed in other faith traditions, in other cultural contexts, will experience their contact with the Divine life in other equally valid ways. Troeltsch is now inclined to say that all the world religions are tending in the same direction. All religion has a common goal in the absolute future and a common ground in the Divine Spirit.

Later scholars have tried to fill out this rather vague relativism with detailed studies of the complementarity to be discerned, particularly between Christianity and the Indian religions. Ninian Smart attempted this in his Gifford Lectures, *Beyond Ideology*,[22] as did John Robinson in his Teape Lectures, *Truth is Two-Eyed*.[23] But the tendencies adumbrated by Troeltsch have found their most thorough development and articulation in John Hick's philosophy of religious pluralism. Now it might be thought that the best way of dealing with the diversity problem which arises when the cumulative case for Christian belief reaches the stage of appeals to the history of religions, and to the experiential and axiological dimensions of this history outlined above, would be to adopt Hick's philosophy of religious pluralism, and to allow each faith tradition to proceed separately with its own case in support of its own total world-view. This would only work if it were shown to be possible and plausible to forswear comparative evaluation in favour of a philosophy of religious pluralism in which the religions of the world, including one's own (in Hick's and my own case, Christianity), are seen as different, historically and culturally shaped 'human responses to the transcendent', to cite the subtitle of Hick's Gifford Lectures, *An Interpretation of Religion*.[24] Hick is not, of course, advocating a single, syncretistic, world religion of the future. Believers will continue to be renewed and sustained in their own faith communities; but, philosophically speaking, they will come to recognize their own world-view as but one among many phenomenal representations of the ineffable, noumenal ultimate, which Hick calls the Real.

The Appeal to History I

This is, as I say, a hugely attractive way of coping with the diversity problem. A cumulative case in support of Christian belief, such as I have been sketching out, begins with cosmological, teleological, and axiological appeals, shared in common with cumulative cases in support of other religious worldviews, the appeals to nature already shading into appeals to history in the way indicated. But, as these appeals shade into appeals to history, the cases branch out in different culturally conditioned, though not ultimately incompatible, directions. A philosophy of religious pluralism, such as Hick's, is required at this point in order to show that the prima-facie incompatibilities are not ultimate. They can all be understood as different phenomenal representations of the life-transforming pressure of the transcendent Real, itself beyond all human conceptualization.

I very much doubt, however, whether this attractive solution to the diversity problem is going to work. Its implausibility from the point of view of a developed Christian theology will emerge more clearly when we consider, as we will in the next two chapters, the more specific appeals to history which support, or even underlie, the Christian doctrines of election and covenant, incarnation, and redemption. Similar objections to the philosophy of religious pluralism would be likely to emerge from other world faiths, each with their own 'jealousies', as John V. Taylor called them.[25]

Hick himself makes some comparative evaluations. He gives the priority to what he calls, following Karl Jaspers, the post-axial religions,[26] the great world religions, each capable of sustaining the faith of millions, and each capable of reconciling its developing tradition with the findings of modern science. The so-called axial age contains a range of major breakthroughs in the history of religions, associated with Confucius and the Taoist scriptures in China, with the Upanishads, the Buddha, and Mahavira in the Indian subcontinent, with Zoroaster in Persia, with the Hebrew prophets in Israel, and with Plato in Greece. The leitmotif of these movements, carried forward within the Semitic stream by Jesus and Muhammad and the rise of Christianity and Islam, and within the Eastern stream by the growth and spread of Mahayana Buddhism, is the soteriological motif, the view that the human condition can be transformed, evil overcome, and spiritual resources drawn on for liberation and renewal. Hick does not disparage the archaic, pre-axial religions; but they cannot, he holds, reach the same level as the post-axial faiths, since they lack these universal, relational, and transformative capacities.

Philosophical objections to Hick's position would include fundamental criticism of the Kantian epistemology adopted by Hick to restrict religious doctrines to the level of phenomenal representations of a strictly unknowable ultimate. The coherence of the claim that 'personae' and 'impersonae' of the Real are equally valid vehicles for representing the transformative power of the Real would have to be challenged. Alvin Plantinga, in *Warranted Christian Belief*,[27] deploys clear and powerful arguments for the unavoidability of ascribing at least some positive predicates to the ultimate. Hick himself speaks of the religions as responses to the pressure or causal efficacy of the Real in bringing about the transformation from ego-centredness to reality-centredness, which is, as I say, the leitmotif of post-axial religion.

But it is worth noting how many factors in the early stages of the cumulative case for Christian belief that occupied us initially, before we began to move on to the developed doctrines of

Christianity and their historical support, require comparative evaluation in favour of theistic metaphysics, and against impersonal monism or a non-theistic Absolute. This is true of both natural theology and what we might call the rudiments of revealed theology. While cosmological arguments might allow neutrality between personal and impersonal transcendence, teleological arguments, like those appealing to the anthropic principle, suggest intention, and thus mind, behind the world process. Axiological arguments, too, as we saw in the case of Mavrodes's moral argument, suggest that, to quote him again, 'things like mind and purpose must be deeper in the real world than they would be in a Russellian world'. While some religious experience, especially in the East and Far East, might be suggestive of impersonal transcendence, much, even there, points to the idea of revelation, not in the sense just of an eye-opening experience, but of a message, a claim, a demand, a gift, from a personal source of love and succour. This is certainly true of the religions of Semitic origin, but also, in many ways, of the recovery of Hinduism in the Indian subcontinent—one thinks of the *Bhagavadgita*, for example—and of the spread of Mahayana Buddhism in the Far East. As we turn to consider the appeals to history involved in Judaeo-Christian religion, the necessity of construing not only revealed theology but also natural theology in terms of *personal* transcendence is undeniable.

But, of course, the theistic religions, while sharing some common features (not least in the sphere of the support given by theistic metaphysics), are very varied in their developed theologies; and their revelation claims, while perhaps in part complementary, often conflict. Christianity's key doctrines of the Incarnation and the Trinity inevitably, unless

76

demythologized, require some 'grading' of religions in terms of their finality and universal scope. Chapters 4 and 5 will explore these issues. My present point is simply that the diversity problem remains. It cannot be resolved simply by adoption of a philosophy of religious pluralism.

Let us now consider how the diversity problem is dealt with by three of the philosophers of religion whose work has been singled out for special attention here: Alvin Plantinga, William Alston, and Robert Adams.

We would not expect to get much help from Plantinga. I commented, in Chapter 2, on Plantinga's theory concerning the internal warrant of a basic belief system such as Christianity, given that potential objections or defeaters have been shown not to bite. And I noted his rejection of the implication that any basic belief system, however crazy, would equally have warrant on his view. But what about non-crazy, non-Christian world-views, whose premises cannot be shown, or be plausibly suggested, to be false? Having refuted the philosophy of religious pluralism, has Plantinga anything to say about the fact of religious pluralism? Well, he makes the fair point that, in most areas of life, people disagree, and some are closer to the truth than others. He also fairly observes that Hick does not produce any argument for the view that no world religion could be closer to the truth than others. He adds the *ad hominem* point that it is no more intolerant to affirm the truth of Christianity than it is to affirm the truth of the philosophy of religious pluralism.[28] None of this gets us very far. But Plantinga returns to the fact of pluralism towards the end of his book when dealing with alleged defeaters,[29] and asks whether a knowledge of the facts of religious pluralism constitutes a defeater for Christian belief. He thinks not, chiefly on the grounds, with which we are already familiar, that, for the convinced believer, there can be no question of epistemic parity between his or her faith stance and that of someone standing within a conflicting basic belief system. Just as my clear recollection of walking on the hills on a certain day makes it impossible for me to concede that I might have been committing a murder somewhere else at that time, no matter what evidence or motive the prosecuting counsel may produce, and even if I cannot prove that I was on the hills, so the committed Christian need not be thrown by the fact of conflicting world-views, even if he cannot demonstrate the truth of his beliefs or the falsity of those of others. For, as Plantinga has argued all along, a set of basic beliefs is not warranted by external arguments appealing to other factors. In its own terms, this position is unassailable. However, I did suggest that it is still vulnerable to collapse, if wholly unsupported; and I now suggest that the fact of real piety and spirituality elsewhere, and of other all-embracing theistic world-views, does infect Plantinga's exclusivism with more than a little implausibility. Once again, Christians may not require arguments for the truth of Christianity for their faith stance to be warranted; but it does help if the truth of Christ, and his finality, can actually be argued for.

So, let us see if William Alston fares any better.[30] Alston admits that the diversity problem is the most difficult problem for his position regarding the epistemology of religious experience. For, unlike sense perception, mystical perception is diverse in the various traditions and contexts of religious faith, and the beliefs it supports are not only different but also incompatible in various important respects. Not in all respects, however. It is quite possible to suppose that the same creative and active Ultimate—in theistic terms, God—underlies and brings about the various faith traditions and the mystical (or religious) experiences of those nurtured in them. But God's basic characteristics are differently conceived, and God's key redemptive actions are very differently conceived and weighted, say, in Christianity, from how they are, say, in Hinduism or Islam. Alston points out that these differences may be accounted for by the relative difficulty of access to truth in these areas, by the pervasively distorting effect of sin, and, most importantly, by the differences in what people have to go on in different streams of history and culture. Alston adopts what he calls a 'worst case scenario' and considers the rationality of Christian mystical perception on the assumption that there are no significant independent reasons for preferring it to its rivals. This puts him firmly in the Plantinga camp, with its emphasis on internal justification. Admittedly, there is more in Alston than in Plantinga on the evidence of the fruits of the Spirit in the lives of the saints, where third-person perceptual justification is concerned, and on experiential confirmation through growth in the Christian life, where first-person justification is concerned. But that Alston is more an Anglican epistemologist than a Reformed one is shown by two factors. In the first place, he is prepared, in ways I have already touched on, to integrate the appeal to experience, both first-person and third-person, with other appeals, to natural theology and to revelation and tradition, in a mutually reinforcing, cumulative case. This means that, in the second place, his worst case scenario is precisely that, a *worst case* scenario. In fact, he thinks 'that much can be done to support a theistic metaphysics, and that something can be done by way of recommending the "evidences of Christianity" '.[31] Sadly, he does not pursue this line in *Perceiving God*, but the words just quoted encourage me to pursue it here.

The Appeal to History I

What about Robert Adams? Adams's discussion of the diversity problem is restricted, given the subject-matter of his book, to the ethical deliverances of what is claimed as special revelation in the various historic religious traditions. Some of these do flatly contradict each other, but others are just different. 'Such possibilities', writes Adams, 'are suggested by the idea of a transcendent Good ever imperfectly imaged in the contingencies of human history.'[32] This notion of a variety of contingent empirical reflections of the Good is important for Adams. 'We learn through the collective experience of human history the possibility and value of various forms of social life.' These forms of life, and individual saintly personalities fostered within them, need not be inconsistent with each other. 'Finite things can resemble God in different ways.' Divine commands too may differ, in different religious contexts, just as vocations may. Of course, Adams admits, I cannot suppose that God has commanded you, a Hindu, to do something that I, a Christian, hold to be evil. But this is a problem that occurs within traditions. It occurs *vis-à-vis* our own sacred Scriptures, as over God's alleged command, in the book of Joshua, to slaughter the inhabitants of Canaan. 'Modern Jews and Christians', says Adams, 'may well find it hard to believe that God really commanded Joshua to practice genocide against the Canaanites, no matter what is written in the Bible.'[33] What Adams goes on to say about ethical development can be extended to doctrinal development, and can be applied inter-religiously as well as intra-religiously. His reply to Bernard Williams's objection that admission of the interplay between ethical and religious development shows that religion is a merely human construct[34] is worth quoting: 'It overlooks the possibility that religion will regard its development as a joint product of human construction and divine guidance.'[35] Adams concludes his reflections on the diversity problem by repeating his suggestion that, subject to the above-mentioned ethical constraints, 'a theistic outlook can appropriately include the idea that God may have guided different people in different directions'.[36]

This takes us much further than Alston, and suggests a much more positive way of regarding other faiths from a Christian perspective. It may, of course, be easier to do this in respect of ethics than in respect of doctrine, especially soteriology. There is, after all, more common ground and scope for complementarity where ethics is concerned, as Hans Küng has urged in the course of his global ethics project.[37] But, as we turn in the next chapter to the topic of appeals to history in support of specifically Christian doctrines of incarnation and redemption, we will need to press the question of how far a positive appreciation of the revelatory and salvific significance of other religions can be embraced within a Christian world-view. Christianity, as Plantinga and Alston insist, has its own internal rational and experiential warrant, but the cumulative case in support of it is strengthened, and better integrated with the other elements in the cumulative case, if it can include a plausible Christian theology of religion and the religions.

Such a theology must contain the following three features: (i) it must account for the diversity of religions; (ii) it must, perhaps along the lines of Adams's treatment, appreciate the value of that diversity; and (iii) it must account for the necessary particularity and indispensability of its own key element: namely, the finality of Christ. Of course, the other faiths have a comparable task: namely, the production of theologies of religion and the religions, each from its own perspective.

Comparative evaluation will entail assessment of the relative success of these enterprises.

That this can be done is shown by an early example of its actually having been done; and I conclude this chapter by returning to H. H. Farmer's *Revelation and Religion*.[38] It will be recalled that Farmer suggests an extension of natural theology to include the rational defence of a theism of incarnation and reconciliation as a coherent world-view, one making most sense of all the data. The bulk of his book consists in an attempt to show how, on the assumption of the truth of Christian incarnational and soteriological belief, it is possible 'to bring the vast and confused multiplicity of religious phenomena into some sort of intelligible order, and to interpret and elucidate them in relation to one another'. To do this, Farmer claims, would be to confirm the truth of the assumption, 'at least to the extent of helping to build up that total Christian philosophy or world view on which its reasoned confirmation must in part rest'.[39]

On Farmer's view, the mass of data thrown up by the history of religions makes most sense in the light of three further assumptions: (i) that there is a common essence underlying all genuinely religious phenomena; (ii) that these phenomena arise at the point where ultimate reality impinges upon the human spirit; and (iii) that all living and essential religion is a matter of God's personal encounter with humanity. These assumptions allow a very positive reading of many strands in the history of religions. Farmer provides much interesting, detailed reflection on the way in which key elements in Christian incarnational and soteriological religion are mirrored, though often distorted, in other contexts, distortions which, of course, also occur in Christian history itself, as in what he calls, citing Calvin himself, the *horribile decretum* of double predestination.

I cannot go into all the details of Farmer's typology of the key elements in religion here. In some ways his work is reminiscent of the earlier Troeltsch, for whom, it will be recalled, Christianity synthesizes a greater range of developmental tendencies in the history of religion than any other religion. Indeed, Troeltsch's notion of synthesis is echoed in Farmer's final chapter on the element of unification in religion. Comparative religion is largely concerned with the different ways in which its leading elements—dependence, idealism, inwardness, obligation, eudaimonism, corporateness, dynamism, withdrawal, and fulfilment—are unified in a total theoretical, practical, and spiritual world-view.

I restrict myself to singling out for special notice one element in Farmer's normative assumption concerning Christianity's incarnational soteriology: namely, the centrality of history. Interestingly he suggests that it might be better to drop the word 'incarnation' in favour of the word 'inhistorization'; for unlike the Hindus' *avatar*, 'a divine being who merely drops into the human scene from the realm of eternity, unheralded, unprepared for, without roots in anything that has gone before in history and without any creative relationship to the unfolding of what comes after', the Christ of Christian faith

is a fully historic, individualized human person, a Jew of the first century, his whole being and life consciously rooted in, and incomprehensible apart from, the continuing history of the covenant people, Israel, and the subsequent history of the new covenant people, the Church; furthermore this history is itself embedded in, inseparable from, incomprehensible except as related to, the wider history of mankind by which it is always in some measure conditioned and which it in turn reciprocally conditions.[40]

This extended quotation sets the scene for the second half of this book. For the cumulative case in support of Christian belief, as it moves beyond natural theology into revealed theology, includes not only appeals to historically formed value systems, including the whole history of religions world-wide, and not only appeals to theologies of religion that attempt to make best sense of the whole history of religions. It also includes appeals to specific historical events that, under certain conditions, invite doctrinal construal in terms of providence, covenant, incarnation, and redemption, including the redemption of the world.

4

The Appeal to History II:
Christ and the Church

CHRISTIAN APOLOGETIC, I have been suggesting, consists in an extended cumulative case argument, appealing to both nature and history. It includes cosmological, teleological, and axiological strands, the latter already embracing appeals to historically and culturally formed faith traditions. We now come to the specific appeals to history that lie at the heart of the Judaeo-Christian tradition and of the Christian religion in particular. For while all developed religions are historical religions, most of them appealing to historical founders and scriptures and to the spiritual, life-transforming power of their teachings, Christianity's teachings are bound up with history in a very special sense. Its spiritual and life-transforming power is held to spring from, and depend on, very special acts of God in history: the formation of a people chosen to be 'a light to the nations', (Isa. 49: 6), the Incarnation of God in person at a particular point in history, the Resurrection of the crucified Messiah, and the formation of a body of witnesses to those acts, itself a developing, and ever more widely ramifying, fact of human history.

Now, clearly, a lot of theology has gone into the way in which I have just characterized the historical foundations of the

Christian faith. Our special interest in this chapter is how far the data of history *per se*—the empirical facts accessible to the historian *qua* historian—can be held to support the theological appraisal of those data as constituting vehicles of revelation and redemption, and how far Christian appeals to history involve the postulation of meta-historical factors.

First, a number of preliminary points. One of the factors to which special attention will have to be paid is the question of the different expectations which one brings, even hypothetically, to the assessment of historical evidence. This is a point to which we shall return in considering Swinburne's treatment of the way in which probability judgements depend, in large part, on background evidence. But already one's expectations about revelation will have been affected by prior factors in the cumulative case. Anyone convinced that theistic metaphysics offers the best explanation of the existence of a universe productive of persons and cultures will have grounds for expecting divine revelation. I said something in the last chapter about the factors in natural theology suggestive of personal explanation, factors requiring explanation in terms of mind, purpose, and action; but it is worth recalling that Thomas Aquinas, in his natural theology, goes much further than this in arguing, on purely rational grounds, for goodness and even love in God. These arguments are explored in detail by Norman Kretzmann in *The Metaphysics of Theism: Aquinas's Natural Theology in Summa Contra Gentiles I.*[1] In the light of these factors, the hypothesis of theism may well give rise to expectations not only of revelation, but also of incarnation. I shall discuss this point when we come to the question of evidence for the Incarnation.

I stress again that this whole approach can be made hypothetically. Prescinding from commitment to theism, one can ask what difference a theistic perspective would make to the assessment of the historical evidence. It will be recalled that Farmer asked us to consider the sense made of the history of religions on the assumption, hypothetically, of a Christian theism of incarnation and reconciliation.[2] The scope and power of the resulting world-view was held to provide some confirmation of that assumption. Similarly, at this stage in the cumulative case, the apologist invites his interlocutor to consider the history of Israel and the story of Jesus, on the assumption of theism. Of course the apologist, in commending the faith, is not himself proceeding hypothetically, but rather inviting such hypothetical reflection from his listeners. What Plantinga says about what he calls 'conditionalization'[3] can be applied the other way round. Just as it is quite possible for the Christian to consider the Bible from a purely historical point of view by putting himself in the shoes of the secular historian, so the latter can consider the evidence from a theistic point of view by putting himself in the believer's shoes. This kind of procedure goes on all the time in the comparative study of religions.

This illustrates the way in which different elements in the cumulative case for Christian belief interact and mutually reinforce one another. Natural theology leads to an expectation of revelation, increasing its prior probability. Historical factors, in themselves just puzzling or at most suggestive of interpretation in terms of divine activity, can be made most sense of on the hypothesis of theism.

The matter of expectations being relative to prior assumptions needs careful handling, of course. In a robust paper on 'The Impact of Scriptural Studies', Michael Dummett says quite rightly that 'Estimates of probability depend crucially on background assumptions. What is probable if there is no God, or if Christ and his disciples were misguided fanatics, becomes quite improbable if Christianity is true'[4]—and vice versa, of course. But Dummett uses this very proper point as a basis for a most uncritical, indeed untheological, assault on biblical criticism. And indeed it is only too easy to use the presumption of theism, to adapt Antony Flew's phrase, to justify pretty well anything, from miracles to fundamentalism. Hensley Henson was extremely wary of relying on prior expectation in handling historical evidence, as Anthony Dyson pointed out in the first series of Hensley Henson Lectures in 1973.[5] Henson had taken issue with William Temple on precisely this issue. I quote from Dyson's book: 'Temple, according to Henson, was saying that if, as Christians we postulate that the ruling power in the universe is a person and that there is unique revelation, complete and final, given at a moment in history, then we shall expect to find what are usually called miraculous occurrences surrounding that unique event.'[6] Henson's objections were partly to do with this approach's riding roughshod over careful historical enquiry, but partly to do with theological incongruities in the assumption that God's way with the world would be that of miraculous intervention. We shall return to this point shortly, when we consider the factors conditioning any appeal to Scripture as evidence.

We must remind ourselves that, in speaking of tentative, probabilistic, even hypothetical argumentation towards the construction of a cumulative case for Christian belief, we are simply concerned with the question of possible *support* for a position occupied and lived by many people with unqualified commitment. I have conceded to Plantinga the rightness of a

Basic Belief Apologetic as far as the internal warrant of Christianity for Christians is concerned. The arguments and the evidences which I am considering here are not foundational in any epistemological sense, even if they pertain to what belongs, ontologically, to the foundations of Christian faith—the Incarnation, for example.

This distinction between experientially confirmed internal warrant, on the one hand, and probabilistic, external support, on the other, enables us to accept with confidence the possibility, discussed by Ian Ramsey in his *On Being Sure in Religion*[7] and by Basil Mitchell in his *Faith and Criticism*,[8] of indeed being sure in religion while being tentative in theology—and, *a fortiori*, being tentative in philosophy of religion. It also enables us to dismiss categorically D. Z. Phillips's amusing version of Psalm 139 as allegedly paraphrased by Swinburne and Mitchell: 'Whither shall I go from thy Spirit? Or whither shall I flee from thy presence? If I ascend up into heaven, it is highly probable' <or cumulatively apparent> 'that thou art there: if I make my bed in hell, behold it is highly probable' <or cumulatively apparent> 'that thou art there also.'[9] Phillips explicitly declares this to be a foundationalist reading of the psalm. But it is perverse of Phillips to take Mitchell, and even Swinburne, that way. The psalmist is giving voice to the unqualified faith position of his convictional community, whose rationality has been analysed by Plantinga. Mitchell and Swinburne, who, I imagine, are perfectly willing and able to sing that psalm without qualification, are exploring possible lines of support for that faith position and possible lines of apologetic in arguing with atheism.

What I say here about non-foundationalist apologetic also applies, as reference to Ian Ramsey's talk of tentative theology shows, to self-critical theological reflection on the basic beliefs of Christianity.

In turning more directly to the role of appeals to the history of Israel and the story of Jesus as integral parts of Christian apologetic, I refer again to the work of Austin Farrer. In Chapter 6 of *Faith and Speculation*,[10] the chapter entitled 'Revelation and History', Farrer offers a highly nuanced account of divine revelation as operating, like divine providence, in and through the all-too-human and fallible strands of human history. For Farrer, sacred history is not some kind of meta-history, like Barth's *Urgeschichte*, lying back of, or beyond, ordinary human history, and thus inaccessible except to the eye of faith. Nor does revelation consist in some pure datum from beyond, such as an infallible book dictated from on high. Rather, human history, in all its messiness and fallibility, is itself the vehicle and medium of God's providential, revelatory, activity. 'Sacred history', writes Farrer, 'is primarily concerned with the actions and fortunes of people in dialogue with God.'[11] 'God reveals himself effectively through fallible minds and takes care that their imperfections shall not frustrate his purpose; for through his continued operation in us he winnows out in us the wheat from the chaff.'[12] For Farrer, the paradigm of God's saving purpose, triumphing in and through the weakness and fallibility of its instruments, is 'Christ's ability to play his part with a mental furniture acquired from his village rabbi'.[13]

God's action, Farrer allows, is not itself part of human history. We can call it 'meta-historical' if we like. But the effects of God's action are there to be seen in human history, in particular in the history of Israel and the story of Jesus, though not only there. The dialogue continues, and we may add, extending Farrer's own view, takes place elsewhere as well.

The Appeal to History II

Putting the matter in my own terms, what I am suggesting here is that certain strands of all-too-human history, which from a purely historical point of view are just puzzling, or at most suggestive, make most sense when seen as embodying, and as revelatory of, God's redemptive purposes.

Farrer's view of historically mediated revelation applies, of course, both to the Scriptures themselves and to the events to which the Scriptures bear witness. The idea of divine–human dialogue in and through the fallible media of history is particularly important for any rational appeal to the Bible. In Christian apologetic, as already pointed out, one does not appeal to the Bible simply as an authority. One appeals, in Coleridge's words from *Confessions of an Inquiring Spirit*,[14] to what 'finds me'—that is, to what comes across as ethically and spiritually profound and life-transforming. That sounds a somewhat subjective criterion; but, of course, it is both inter-subjective in its formation and cognitive in its implications. It is a matter of communally formed doxastic practice, as Alston showed in respect of its experiential connotations, and as Adams showed in respect of its ethical connotations.

The dialogue model, whereby the teacher is understood to work with the pupil at the level which the pupil has reached at any stage, was used by Mitchell in the final chapter of his *The Justification of Religious Belief*,[15] and has been developed in great detail and with great insight by David Brown, in his two books *Tradition and Imagination*[16] and *Discipleship and Imagination*.[17] Brown shows how divine revelation is best seen as mediated through a process of growth and development in Jewish and Christian response to the events and interpretations recorded in the Scriptures. At every stage, including that of the Incarnation, to which I shall turn shortly, there is divine accommodation to the human context and condition at the time, and then a long process of imaginative appropriation, with much backsliding as well as enhancement of understanding and practice. Of particular interest, in the light of our reflections in the last chapter on the history of religions, is Brown's demonstration of how Christians can learn from Judaism as it has continued to develop, and from Islam.

Some such approach is surely required if we are to come to terms with the fact of much primitive and unethical material in the Scriptures themselves. In one of his last essays, 'Shall Not the Judge of all the Earth Do What Is Just?',[18] Norman Whybray drew attention to the 'dark' side of God as portrayed in the Hebrew Scriptures: the death and destruction wrought upon the Egyptians, the genocide practised against the inhabitants of Canaan, the hideously excessive punishments inflicted on the Israelites themselves, the testing of Abraham and Job, to say nothing of the bears sent to ravage forty-two insolent boys in 2 Kings 2. The story of Abraham and Isaac was famously wrestled with by Kierkegaard in *Fear and Trembling*; but Kierkegaard's thesis about 'the teleological suspension of the ethical', the thesis that ethical norms can at times be overridden by the higher purposes of God, fails to commend itself to the majority of ethicists, secular or Christian.[19] Nor are such problems restricted to what Christians call the Old Testament. No lectionary for Matins or Evensong would ever prescribe Acts 5: 1–11 for the second lesson, the grotesque and superstitious story of Ananias and Sapphira being made to drop dead for withholding some of the proceeds of the sale of their property. I stress again the point made by Robert Adams against Bernard Williams. Ethical criticism of the Scriptures is not destructive of their use in Judaism or Christianity. Ethical and religious development can indeed be thought of as a joint product of human construction and divine guidance.'

Reverting to the Hebrew Scriptures, we can only express gratitude to historical criticism for showing how much human, relatively primitive construction has gone into their making, and for recognition that the actual history of the Patriarchal times, of the Exodus, and of the settlement up to the monarchy, is largely inaccessible *wie es eigentlich gewesen* (as it actually was), to cite Leopold von Ranke's famous phrase.[20] It is worth noting, however, that, according to Richard Evans, in his book *In Defence of History*,[21] the word *eigentlich* in the quoted phrase is often misunderstood. Ranke was not just interested in bare facts. *Eigentlich* would be better translated 'essentially' rather than 'actually', and that might well open up doors to meta-historical interpretation.

If the scriptural record is so messy and ambiguous, what is it that we are 'actually' appealing to when, in the cumulative case for Christian belief, we appeal to the history of Israel? Well, in the first place, we appeal to what is also appealed to in a cumulative case for Jewish belief: namely, the formation, however messily, of a people convinced of, and committed to, a special role in history, that of being faithful to God's call and to God's promise, and of bearing witness to God's faithfulness through good and ill. Their developing ethical monotheism, as we see it coming to expression in the later prophets, with their call to holiness and justice, in the Wisdom literature and especially in the Psalms, with their expression of the love of God and of God's law, is itself best seen, it is suggested, as a vehicle of special revelation within the history of religions. This is perhaps most notably the case with respect to two particularly striking features of Israelite religion: recognition and acceptance of the idea of redemptive suffering, and development of a linear view of universal history, within a framework of eschatological hope. In all these respects Israel was called to be 'a light to the nations', and, as we shall see, that call remains.

Christianity, of course, sees the history of Israel as also constituting, and from its own point of view *primarily* constituting, God's preparation of the context and conditions for the Incarnation. As I have written elsewhere in an essay on 'The Jewishness of Jesus',

the genuine humanity of the incarnate Lord did not only have to be particular, limited, and historically and culturally conditioned, as all humanity is. It had to be *thus* limited in the specifically Jewish way in which Jesus's humanity was limited. For only a Jew, with a Jew's inheritance, a Jew's faith and understanding and a Jew's hope, could be God incarnate. That faith alone could sustain the very image of God's being. It was, so Christians believe, for that purpose that God, in his providence, fashioned the Jewish way of being human and the Jewish way of being religious.[22]

An immediate caveat is called for. Christians cannot say that it was only for that purpose, preparation for the Incarnation, that God chose the Jews. A credible Christian apologetic must distance itself from the old idea of supersession, the idea that the new covenant simply replaced the old. Just as the role of the whole history of religions *vis-à-vis* the formation of the Judaeo-Christian tradition does not abrogate their independent validity and value, so Judaism's role in preparing for the Incarnation does not abrogate its validity and value as recipient of the covenant and as a 'light to the nations'. This was already clear, although 'clear' is perhaps not quite the right word, to St Paul in Romans 9–11, and it was reaffirmed in the Second Vatican Council's *Nostra Aetate*: 'the Jews remain most dear to God because of their fathers, for He does not repent of the gifts He makes nor of the calls He issues.'[23]

These reflections do not, of course, resolve the issue between Jews and Christians over whether the Messiah has come, or whether Jesus of Nazareth was indeed more than a prophet. But they do reinforce the point that an overarching purpose in the divine economy, focused in the Incarnation, does not exclude the possibility, or even the necessity, if God is love, of recognizing a variety of revelatory and salvific channels in world history, or a special lasting significance in the people and the faith that made the Incarnation possible.

James Barr, in Chapter 17 of *The Concept of Biblical Theology*,[24] a chapter entitled 'Judaism after Biblical Times', notes how Christian Old Testament scholars have come to reject the largely negative picture of post-biblical Judaism that was to be found in the work of Walther Eichrodt and Gerhard von Rad. He raises the question of the theological significance of the fact that Jesus appeared on the scene not within the time span of the Hebrew Scriptures themselves but 'only after there has been a time of ripening or maturation'. In other words, the importance of the developing post-biblical Jewish tradition is already a factor to be reckoned with in Christian incarnational theology. This raises the possibility of continuing cross-fertilization between the developing traditions of Christianity and Judaism. It is noteworthy how Barr concludes his whole book with a strong endorsement of David Brown's work, in *Tradition and Imagination*, on continuing revelation and on Christians learning from Judaism and Islam, to which I have already referred.

All this may appear to be leading us back to a philosophy of religious pluralism. But we have not yet reckoned with the main factor in a cumulative case for Christian belief that makes Christianity resistant to such a philosophy: namely, the evidence for the Incarnation. I doubt, in any case, if Judaism would rest content with a philosophy of religious pluralism, despite its endorsement by the Chief Rabbi in a short article in *The Times.* Jonathan Sacks, writing in the aftermath of the terrorist attack on New York on 11 September 2001, averred that cultures and religions claiming universal truth are bound to clash with terrible consequences, not least for the Jews. Whereas on his view 'the glory of the human world is diversity', 'The true moral universals are few and exist to protect cultural and religious difference: the sanctity of human life, the dignity of the human person, and the freedom we need to be true to ourselves and a blessing to others.' 'God no more wants all faiths and cultures to be the same than a loving parent wants his or her children to be the same.'[25] I leave it to our Jewish colleagues to say whether this does justice to Judaism's understanding of its own role *vis-à-vis* the nations, or to Judaism's own conception of history and eschatology. I return to the whole question of universal history in the last chapter.

But now we must consider the question of evidence for the Incarnation. The full cumulative case for Christian belief is certainly going to appeal to the Incarnation, at a particular point in history, of God the Son, for our sake and for our salvation. Much of the case will concern the moral and religious significance and power of a theism of incarnation and reconciliation, to cite Farmer's phrase yet again. I shall summarize what this means in the next chapter. But how much of this appeal is strictly an appeal to history? How much actual historical evidence is there to support the interpretation of incarnational Christology? Well, granted that assessments of the evidence will differ according to one's prior expectations and the background evidence that one acknowledges, the evidence itself consists in a great deal more than the negative truth conditions of the doctrine already mentioned. I have already admitted that incarnational Christology would collapse if it could be shown that Jesus never existed, was a reprobate, or was not crucified. It would collapse if it could be shown that Jesus was not raised from the dead; although, here, the boundary between the historical and the meta-historical has to be pondered. And it would collapse if the story of Jesus had had no effect in history whatsoever, or was incapable of being appropriated, inwardly and communally, as in fact it has been, over the centuries, in the lives of Christians and in the sacramental fellowship of the Church. In the last chapter I shall be pursuing the question of whether there are, or even must be, further effects to be discerned more widely in world history.

Already the negative truth conditions of incarnational Christology can be seen to include what is in fact highly positive evidence in its support. Let us build up the picture again, concentrating on the positive side. Appeal is made to the life and teaching of Jesus as recorded in the Gospels. On any reckoning, we have here the picture of an extraordinarily penetrating and authoritative teacher and prophet. Historical criticism has disclosed much theological interpretation and some legendary embellishment in the Gospel records; and, while it is hard to assess the miraculous element, it is hard to deny that in Jesus of Nazareth we have to do with a charismatic healer. Even the agnostic historian E. P. Sanders, in *The Historical Figure of Jesus*,[26] presents us with a figure who, while every inch a Jew, nevertheless stands out remarkably from his Jewish background. But the story of Jesus, from the cradle to the grave, intensely moving as is the account of his passion and death, as any listener to Bach's *St Matthew Passion* would agree, is not, by itself, going to require incarnational Christology for its interpretation, were it not for what came after his death on the Cross. And there is no doubt that appeals to history as an integral part of Christian apologetic will include, above all things, appeal to the Resurrection of Jesus Christ from the dead.

As I say, this is more than a merely historical appeal. The historian *qua* historian can only point to the claimed appearances of the risen Christ and to the empty tomb tradition. As Sanders puts it: 'That Jesus' followers (and later Paul) had resurrection experiences is, in my judgement, a fact. What the reality was that gave rise to the experiences I do not know.'[27] Sanders does not mention the empty tomb tradition at this point, but I think it has to be reckoned with, as well as the appearances tradition, for the reasons given by Pannenberg in the second volume of his *Systematic Theology*.[28] Pannenberg, of course, does not view these puzzling facts from an agnostic perspective, as Sanders does. But the question of their best explanation depends very much, as I say, on prior expectations and on evaluation of their consequences. The transformation of the disciples from demoralized fugitives to preachers of a new age and the emergence and spread of the Christian movement are all historical facts to which appeal is made in Christian apologetic. In connection with the other elements in the cumulative case to which I have alluded, developed Christian doctrine attempts, among other things, to offer the best explanation of these puzzling historical facts.

The Appeal to History II

I now propose to examine the way in which these matters have been handled by two contemporary philosophers of religion: David Brown, in Chapter 3 of *The Divine Trinity*, the chapter entitled 'Incarnation: The Argument from History', and Richard Swinburne, in Chapter 10 of *The Christian God*, the chapter entitled 'The Evidence of Incarnation'. In each case I shall take account of these authors' more recent work.

Brown begins his chapter by emphasizing the extent to which the persuasiveness of its conclusions will be dependent on arguments employed earlier in his book in favour of an interventionist, rather than a deistic, account of divine activity, and in favour of revelation as divine–human dialogue over time.[29] This reinforces my own recognition of how acceptance of earlier stages in the cumulative case for Christian theism is bound to affect assessment of appeals to history. Interestingly, in his more recent writings, Brown qualifies the first of the points just made, in so far as he now rejects the term 'intervention' and prefers a non-miraculous conception of divine providence, a conception more consonant with his dialogue model, substituting the term 'interaction' for 'intervention'. I shall return to this question when I come to assess the evidential force of appeal to the Resurrection of Jesus.

Brown points out that, on his dialogue model of divine action and divine revelation, there is no problem regarding incarnational Christology being a relatively late development in the apostolic and sub-apostolic age. On the contrary, such growth of insight is what one would expect. On the other hand, there are a number of minimum conditions for the plausibility of such development, and their nature is bound to be controversial. Brown proceeds to examine the evidence in three stages, appealing to the life of Jesus, the Resurrection events, and post-Resurrection reflection.

Where the life of Jesus is concerned, Brown restricts himself to what he calls 'the minimum conditions which must be fulfilled...to justify a subsequent postulation of divinity'.[30] These do not include, according to Brown, Jesus' consciousness of his own divinity. Indeed, Brown suggests that it is doubtful whether a human mind (and incarnational doctrine requires a genuinely human mind) *could* be conscious of its own divinity. There is a stark contrast here with the views of Michael Dummett, who, in his aforementioned paper, declares categorically: 'It remains that there would be no reason to believe him [Jesus] to be God unless he knew himself to be and gave us, through the Apostles, reason to think he knew himself to be.'[31] A comparison between Dummett's assertion here and Brown's more careful reflections reveals a certain theological crudity in Dummett's position that Christian apologetic would do better to forswear. For Brown, it is enough if historical scholarship can point to the unparalleled authority with which Jesus taught and acted, his moral character (Brown speaks of his moral perfection, but that must surely be more of a subsequent theological postulation), and his remarkable intimacy with God the Father (this intimacy explaining, of course, the unparalleled authority with which he spoke and acted).

Where the Resurrection events are concerned, Brown insists that their effect in ratifying Jesus' divinity did not have to be immediate (he distances himself from Pannenberg on this); but he does endorse the view that to affirm their objectivity makes better sense of the evidence than any naturalistic explanation. Interestingly, Brown does not think the empty tomb a necessary condition of such objectivity, although he remains inclined to accept its historicity. The immediate effect of the appearances, understood as objective in the sense of having been caused by their object, was, according to Brown, not an incarnational Christology, but an exaltation Christology, the conviction that the risen Christ was now at God's right hand. Only in the light of the third stage, post-Resurrection reflection, were the early Christians led, eventually, to affirm Christ's divinity.

The suggestion that this was a gradual process is, of course, entirely consonant with Brown's divine–human dialogue model of revelation. On this view, it can be conceded that the early *kerygma*—that is, the early Christian proclamation—spoke only in functional terms of what God had done in Christ. Incarnational doctrine was, at this stage, at most implicit. What made it explicit, by the time of the fourth Gospel, for example, was not so much experience of the risen Christ in the worship of the church, as recognition of the saving power of Christ and the universal dominion of Christ, powers requiring the status of divinity. It was but a small step to read this status back into the earthly life of Jesus (its character, of course, having to be compatible with such a reading) and then, inevitably, even further back into the ascription of pre-existence. Brown concludes his chapter by extending the argument to validate the eventual patristic affirmation of equality of status of the Father and the Son, a process entirely in line with Brown's more recently expounded conception of continuing revelation.[32]

I turn now to Swinburne's chapter, 'The Evidence of Incarnation'.[33] Swinburne too begins with the question of theistic expectation. While it was not necessary, even for atonement, for God to become incarnate (Swinburne here sides with Aquinas against Anselm), there are, nevertheless, good reasons for

God to become incarnate: it would be appropriate for the Creator to identify himself with the creatures he has made in his image; it would teach the dignity of human nature; it would reveal the extent of God's love (Swinburne refers to Kierkegaard's parable of the king and the humble maiden at this point: in order to woo the humble maiden without overawing her with royal panoply, the king puts on peasant's clothes, goes to her village, and woos her incognito); it would show an exemplary human life; it would enable uniquely authoritative teaching; and it would manifest God's willingness to subject himself to the suffering and evil which creation entails. Swinburne refrains from endorsing Duns Scotus against Aquinas regarding the supposition that God would have become incarnate even if humanity had never sinned (unlike Austin Farrer, who opined: 'Christ would still have come to transform human hope, and to bring men into a more privileged association with their Creator than they could otherwise enjoy'[34]).

Granted some such reasons for expecting an incarnation, Swinburne then asks what would show that it had indeed occurred in Jesus Christ. Requisite evidence would certainly include the kind of life and teaching suggestive of divine revelation; but it would also require miraculous confirmation by something like the Resurrection. It would further require pretty rapid recognition by Christ's commissioned church that these data are best interpreted in terms of incarnation. The remainder of his chapter seeks to show the relative inadequacy of alternative explanations of the evidence.

Much of the interest of Swinburne's relatively brief treatment of the evidence for the Incarnation lies in his placing it within the framework of probability theory. More than any other philosopher of religion, Swinburne has applied the skills of formal probability logic to the evidence for theism, the evidence for the Incarnation, and the evidence for the Resurrection. Indeed, in *The Resurrection of God Incarnate*,[35] he presents us with an analysis, in terms of Bayes's theorem, that claims to show that, if background evidence includes not only traditional theism but incarnational Christology, then the probability of the Resurrection is very high indeed. Swinburne actually gives it the figure of 0.97! Taking precise numerical figures with a pinch of salt, I will attempt to discuss this approach rather more informally.

One of the intriguing things about Swinburne's developing views on these matters is the way in which he shows how the more background evidence one brings to the assessment of the historical evidence the less weight the historical evidence by itself has to bear. It has to have some degree of positive strength, of course. And, as I have already remarked, negative truth conditions do not suffice. The main lines of the Gospel narrative have to be taken as veridical. But it is the background evidence and prior expectations that encourage us to take them as veridical. In Swinburne's earlier book, *Revelation*, the background evidence giving prior probability to the Resurrection was the need for revelation and its authentication which serious theism entails.[36] In *The Christian God*, it is not just theism that provides background evidence, but there being some good reasons for expecting an incarnation. This finds confirmation both in the life and teaching of Jesus and in its authentication by the Resurrection.[37] In the book on the Resurrection, Swinburne shows how, given theism and given good reasons for God to become incarnate, then the available evidence of Jesus' life and teaching, together with its uniqueness and the unparalleled appearances and empty tomb traditions, makes it very probable indeed that the Resurrection actually happened.

There are two immediate difficulties that come to mind when confronted with this approach. In the first place, are we not in danger of falling foul of Henson's objection to William Temple which I mentioned earlier in this chapter? Appeal to prior expectations raised by the assumption of incarnational theism might seem to justify uncritical acceptance of all the Gospel miracles and indeed those of Church tradition down the ages. In the second place, is there not a blatant circularity in appealing to the Resurrection as proof of or support for the Incarnation and to the Incarnation as background evidence for the Resurrection?

I will discuss these difficulties in reverse order. The circularity is, I think, only apparent. No one is suggesting that the first disciples entertained prior expectations of either incarnation or resurrection. As David Brown points out, the Resurrection apparently took them completely by surprise, although, without Jewish belief in the general resurrection at the Last Day, they could hardly have made sense of it when it happened. Only gradually did it and its aftermath give rise to a fully incarnational Christology. It is we who, reflecting much later, perhaps only hypothetically, on the question of supporting arguments for the belief system of developed Christianity, can come to appreciate the mutually reinforcing nature of the logic of incarnational Christology and the evidence for the Resurrection as elements in the cumulative case for Christian belief.

The issue of belief in miracles in general is a much more complex matter. It will be recalled that Henson's objection to Temple's idea that there is an expectation of miracles implied in incarnational theism was partly to do with theological incongruities in the assumption that God's way with the world would be that of miraculous intervention. How are we to assess this objection? Well, the *possibility* of miraculous intervention, given theism, is beyond doubt. Hume's main critique of belief in miracles has no force whatsoever, as J. Houston, in *Reported Miracles*,[38] and Alvin Plantinga, in *Warranted Christian Belief*,[39] have shown. Accumulated evidence for what happens normally is totally irrelevant to the question of whether abnormal intervention by God, for good reasons, ever takes place. The other objections made by Hume and by Troeltsch— namely, that miracle stories abound in all religious cultures and especially among the ignorant and unsophisticated—have some force. Admittedly, as Keith Ward points out,[40] the idea that miracle stories in different religions tend to undermine each other's credibility has force only in the context of an exclusivist view of one's own religion. If other religions are themselves recognized as channels of divine activity and revelation, then the notion of miracles elsewhere is perfectly intelligible.

Theologically sensitive objection to miracles, however, includes at least three strands. In the first place, a mature theology has to take account of scientific knowledge and relate its understanding of God's way with the world to modern knowledge about the manner in which the created world operates. In the second place, the problem of evil requires recognition of the reasons why God has to respect the structures of his creation. As Bishop David Jenkins insisted, if direct intervention, with laser beam precision, were a real possibility, its absence in innumerable cases of horrendous evil is morally inexplicable.[41] And thirdly, a theologically sensitive understanding of divine providence operating in and through the law-governed, yet open and flexible, structures of the world makes more sense of the history of religions, and indeed of incarnation, than the postulation of direct, unmediated intervention. (We recall David Brown's later preference for the terminology of 'inter-action' over that of 'intervention'.) It was for these reasons that I suggested that we should think of God's action in the world as a matter of mediated providence, of action, that is, in and through creaturely agencies and energies, rather than the miraculous violation of nature.

These arguments, however, do not, and cannot, apply to the Resurrection. One of the few defects of Houston's *Reported Miracles* is its defence of the credibility of miracle reports in general, in the interests of defence of belief in the Resurrection. But the Resurrection, as Austin Farrer put it, 'is not a miracle like any other. It is a unique manifestation within this world of the transition God makes for us out of this way of being into another.'[42] The integrative intelligibility of the Resurrection in the context of Christian incarnational theism demands exceptional treatment for this element in the story. The way in which God grants an anticipatory manifestation of the transformation of the old creation into the new is not a paradigm for the understanding of God's action in history. It has effects in history (the appearances and the empty tomb); but, as already argued, the event itself is, in the nature of the case, meta-historical.

We may contrast this with the question of appeal to the Virgin Birth, or, more strictly, the virginal conception, of Jesus, as part of the evidence for the Incarnation. I have deliberately omitted consideration of this element, despite its featuring in the chapters by Brown and Swinburne discussed above.[43] Both Brown and Swinburne, like Karl Barth, reject the view that the Incarnation requires a virginal conception. Both recognize the relative weakness of the actual historical evidence compared with that for the Resurrection; but both are inclined to accept its veracity as a God-given sign that Jesus came to us from the side of God. The same is true of Keith Ward's treatment in a curious pamphlet entitled *Evidence for the Virgin Birth*.[44] But it may be thought more theologically appropriate to hold that God did not have to violate the structures of creation in order to enter it in person and unite it to himself by way of incarnation, even if the structures did have to be, if not violated, then transformed beyond nature in order to effect resurrection to the life of the world to come. As such, the Resurrection's purely physical nature is open to theological dispute. Swinburne himself rejects the idea that we have to do here with a resuscitation; and Brown, though accepting the empty tomb tradition, denies its necessity for an objective Resurrection. It is certainly consonant with the givenness of this manifestation within history of the transition out of this way of being, to use Farrer's terminology again, that the empty tomb tradition is veridical. And there are arguments for this, as Pannenberg has shown.[45]

Appeals to history, then, do constitute an integral part of Christian apologetic, and indeed of critical reflection in support of the Christian faith. But, I repeat, these tentative, exploratory, probabilistic, even hypothetical, reasonings do not belong to the foundations of Christianity. Committed participation in the convictional community of the Christian Church has its own internal warrant, as Plantinga says. Christian belief is undoubtedly founded, if true, on God's action in history, most particularly in the Incarnation and the Resurrection. This conviction belongs to the basic belief structure of Christianity as a lived religion. But probabilistic, evidentialist, cumulative reasoning of the sort examined in this book may also be helpful for answering doubts and commending the faith to others. Without any such support, individual Christians might well be vulnerable to loss of faith, and the Church's apologetic would have to be replaced simply by proclamation. Not that there is anything wrong with proclamation. All I am claiming is that there is a place for reasoning, irrespective of commitment, too.

The differentiation, emphasized throughout this book, between the internal warrant of a basic belief structure, on the one hand, and tentative cumulative support, on the other, also allows us to see why individual Christians, while justified internally and experientially, in their basic credal beliefs, may at the same time be agnostic about the details, or indeed quite wrong about some theoretical and practical aspects of their faith. Many Christians, while rightly convinced of the salvific efficacy of the Christ event, may at the same time gravely misconstrue the doctrine of atonement. Equally, many Christians, while rightly convinced of the priority of the theological virtues of faith, hope, and love, may be quite wrong in their attitudes to homosexuality. More to the point, where appeals to history are concerned, many Christians, while rightly convinced of God's culminating revelatory and salvific acts in the history of Israel and the story of Jesus, may be quite wrong in their attitudes to other religions or in their beliefs about the necessity of the Virgin Birth.

In the next chapter I turn from a posteriori, historical considerations to look at what I have called the inner rationale of specifically Christian doctrine. For the cumulative case for Christian belief consists not only of supportive evidence, but also of reflection on the logic and the power of Christian doctrine: its power, that is, to interpret and illuminate what has happened in the past, our present situation, and our future. Then, in the last chapter, I shall return to the subject of history and ask whether there is not a further appeal to be fed into the cumulative case from consideration of universal history and the impact of the Christ event upon the world. Can it be claimed that history contains evidence or signs of the sanctification of the world?

5

A Case for Incarnational and Trinitarian Belief

I HAVE been suggesting in this book that a cumulative case for Christian belief, in moving from the sphere of natural theology to that of revealed theology, will first involve an argument for taking certain historical phenomena as specially revelatory. Such an argument was adumbrated in the last two chapters. The next step will be to argue that the doctrines developed over time in order to make best sense of those historical phenomena themselves contribute to the cumulative case, in so far as their logic, their scope, and their power provide us with the most theoretically and existentially convincing account of where we are, of what is to be done, and of what we may hope for. In this chapter I attempt to sketch the way in which, in Farrer's words, the exposition of these doctrines contributes to their justification.

But first, a little more needs to be said about the way in which natural theology enhances the probability of revelation. The notion of revelation does not in itself presuppose a revealer. We speak of many different types of insight and experience as 'revelations'. 'Travelling cross country to the Far East was a revelation to me,' one might say. In the very early Hindu tradition, *sruti*, translated 'revelation', is more the result of mystical penetration into the mysteries of non-duality than a message from on high. But in the theistic religions, the idea of revelation does entail that of a revealer. And, as I have been urging, it is not unreasonable to suppose that if there is an infinite mind and will behind the whole world process, then that mind will be likely to make itself known to God's personal, rational creatures one way or another. In the first instance this may well take the form of general revelation, the disclosure of God's reality and something of God's nature in and through the things that he has made. General revelation may be correlated with the results of the kind of theistic metaphysics argued for in Chapter 1. In other words, natural theology itself may be held to point to what is in fact God's general revelation. But it is surely most unlikely that a Creator God would restrict himself to such indirect communication. As we have seen in the last two chapters, the history of revelation-claims in the theistic religions is by no means restricted to factors accessible to the human mind at any time or place; and theology is far from being restricted to natural theology. For the most part, theologies are built up, transmitted, and developed within particular historical communities and traditions, responding to much more specific, alleged *special* revelations. As already pointed out, in this sense one cannot speak of theology in general. One is speaking of Jewish theology, Christian theology, Muslim theology, Hindu theology, Sikh theology, Baha'i theology, or whatever. And at this stage, the diversity problem looms very large indeed.

But a number of factors serve to mitigate the apparent arbitrariness of appeals to special revelation. The first is the point just made: it is perfectly reasonable to suppose that, if there is a God, it is likely that he will have made himself known much more specifically than just through general revelation. It is probable that there are much more specific purposes— salvific purposes, for instance—requiring more specific revelation and action *vis-à-vis* the intended consummation of the whole creative process. In the second place, such purported special revelations, if they are going to contribute to the kind of cumulative case under consideration here, are unlikely to be matters just of esoteric information, inaccessible elsewhere, imparted to isolated individuals. Only a claimed revelation that has actually led to a sustained tradition of interpretation, capable of yielding enhanced understanding and new patterns of life and hope, will be worth taking seriously. In the third place, the alleged *locus* of God's special revelation may well be a specific developing tradition of faith and understanding, rather than a one-off impartation of information, and there may well be good reasons for the choice of such an extended vehicle of special revelation. Or else the *locus* of special revelation may be a personal presence of the divine, which, in the nature of the case, requires a particular historical context to be formed and developed for its realization. We shall shortly be exploring the logic of Christian incarnational doctrine in this connection. In the fourth place, there may, contrary to first impressions, turn out to be commonalities between alleged special revelations, just as we saw that there were between different theistic metaphysics or natural theologies. There may be a number of common disclosures, or complementary disclosures, discernible through the disciplines of comparative theology.

That there are indeed such commonalities between a range of specific revelation-claims has been shown by Keith Ward in his four books of comparative theology.[1] These books constitute an impressive foray into comparative theology by a skilled philosopher and theologian. The first, *Religion and Revelation*, explores four scriptural traditions: Judaism, Vedanta (the central Hindu tradition), Buddhism, and Islam, as well as Christianity not so much as a fifth scriptural tradition but rather as a focus of revelation through historical self-manifestation. This allows Ward to develop a non-exclusive view of the Incarnation as the climactic revelation of divine love.

Ward's second book, *Religion and Creation*, shows how four major theologians in the Jewish, Christian, Muslim, and Hindu traditions, Abraham Heschel, Karl Barth, Mohammad Iqbal, and Aurobindo Ghose, have each modified classical, absolutist theism in the direction of a more dynamic, interactionist conception of the divine. Admittedly, Ward is more persuasive on the relation between such a dynamic theology of God and the world as seen in modern science than he is on the specifics of Christian trinitarian theology. Here his doubts over social Trinitarianism lead him to suggest that some creation or other is necessary to God, a view that is undoubtedly alien to most Christian theologians. Ward's view on this will be challenged later in this chapter.

Ward's third book, *Religion and Human Nature*, compares the anthropologies, soteriologies, and eschatologies of the major world religions, bringing out differences as well as common motifs. He admits the difficulty of securing any unified view of truth in these areas; but, just because of their importance for fundamental issues of meaning and destiny, he defends the task of pursuing truth as fairly and comprehensively as possible from within one's own tradition, but in conversation with others and with readiness to learn from other traditions.

The fourth book, *Religion and Community*, surveys the social teachings of five world religions, stressing the importance of religion for social formation and envisaging a global community of many faiths and cultures, in which each makes its distinctive contribution. In discussing the Christian contribution, Ward echoes Paul Tillich in seeing every age of history as the sphere of the Spirit's enabling and transforming work, but goes beyond Tillich in seeing the ultimate meaning and fulfilment of history in the eschatological Kingdom of God.

There is much to be said for the pursuit of such comparative theology. But there is also a case for exploring, and feeding into the cumulative case, what I called the inner rationale of a particular developed theistic religion such as Christianity. In Christianity's case, this can clearly be seen to be operative even in the theology of Karl Barth and in the so-called Reformed Epistemology of Alvin Plantinga. Plantinga's negative apologetics, defending a Christian world-view assumed as basic against charges of incoherence, is rational through and through.[2] But, as was stressed in Chapter 2, there is no reason to restrict such argumentation to negative apologetics alone. The case for further explication of that world-view's logic, scope, and power is very strong. It can be argued, for example, that Christian theology offers not only the best explanation of our being in the world, but also the best diagnosis of the human predicament and its resolution, and the best prognostication of the world's and our ultimate future. In other words, given the negative apologetic—given, for instance, a plausible theodicy, showing how suffering and evil are unavoidable if God is to respect the structures of creation and refrain from overriding human free will—it is quite reasonable to claim that the whole Christian story, as spelled out in systematic and philosophical theology, makes better sense of everything.

In this sense it is still possible to think of Christian theology as the queen of the sciences (at least in the broad sense of a science as a sphere of knowledge) precisely because it explores, and yields much insight into, all aspects of reality. These include not only something of the nature of the mind and heart of love behind the whole world story, but also something of the given nature and ultimate purpose of that story. And, as far as humanity's part in that story is concerned, Christian theology claims to discern both what it is that has gone wrong with the world and what it is that enables its transformation and renewal. As I say, it also claims to discern what the transformed human world is heading towards. I stress again that while the sources of Christian theology are revelation and experience, its tools are those of critical rationality.

The larger part of this book is concerned with the theoretical side of theology, with the rationality of both natural and revealed theology and of the world-view that emerges from these disciplines. But clearly the nature of theology's primary object—namely, the divine and its relationship to everything else—requires us to consider other dimensions of the Christian religion—its practical dimension, for example (that is to say, its ethical consequences and its demands for personal and social renewal)—and also, of course, the dimensions of religious experience, spirituality, and worship, and much else of a highly evaluative nature. Indeed, there can be no fact–value distinction where the world-view of Christianity is concerned. If God is love, value is basic to the nature of things; and the whole universe is designed to evolve the good, the beautiful, and the true, and to culminate eventually in a perfected fellowship mirroring the divine.

Incarnational and Trinitarian Belief

Now all these dimensions of reality are open to rational scrutiny by the reflective theologian, as a number of examples will show. On the cognitive force of religious experience, I refer to the opening chapters of Austin Farrer's *Faith and Specula-tion*,[3] where he writes of the experiential verification of a rationally articulated and defended faith. I have already made use of the full-scale study of religious experience by William Alston in his *Perceiving God.*[4] Alston's case for taking religious experience as seriously as sense experience and treating it as appropriate material for the social formation of beliefs is extremely persuasive, as is Alvin Plantinga's case, in *Warranted Christian Belief*,[5] for including the internal operation of the Holy Spirit among the belief-producing factors in a person whose cognitive faculties are functioning properly according to God's design plan. Not that the Holy Spirit should be thought of as an extra factor alongside the belief-producing powers with which we were originally created. The divine Spirit, as Plantinga himself admits, works in and through our God-given powers, including our reason.

Where spirituality and worship are concerned, I mention two books, Patrick Sherry's *Spirit and Beauty*[6], already referred to in Chapter 3, and Ninian Smart's *The Concept of Worship*,[7] as examples of the way in which one can philosophize about these dimensions, which are undoubtedly just as central to a Christian world-view as those of belief and practice.

Something has already been said about practice in speaking of the personal and social transformations enabled and required by the one of whom Christian soteriology speaks. It is obvious that Christian theology cannot be restricted to discernment of the nature of things as they are. It is as much concerned with Lenin's question, 'What is to be done?', and with the resources available to humankind for at least the partial realization of God's Kingdom here on Earth. Inspiration to energize such practical commitment comes not only from Christian soteriology, but also from Christian eschatology, as Jürgen Moltmann's theological endeavours have shown.[8]

Important as these spiritual and practical aspects of Christianity are, I concentrate, for the remainder of this chapter, on the more theoretical aspects of all these dimensions of Christian doctrine. It will be recalled that H. H. Farmer, in *Revelation and Religion*, argued for what he called 'a theism of incarnation and reconciliation' as offering a more comprehensive world-view than can be found elsewhere.[9] This is a matter of showing not only the coherence of incarnational and trinitarian theology but also the scope and power of Christology, trinitarian theology, Christian soteriology, and Christian eschatology to make sense of the world, its products, and its destiny, when seen as the triune God's creative enterprise.

The logic, scope, and power of these four key elements in Christian doctrine will now be explored, in summary form, in order to illustrate the way in which such exploration can contribute to a cumulative case for Christian belief.

The first two elements—that is, Christology and trinitarian theology—bring us to the heart of what makes Christianity unique. Whatever the Christian faith may share with other theistic religions, and however positive a role it may accord to other world faiths, its conviction of the divinity of Christ and its conviction of the triune nature of God yield a world-view in these respects incommensurable with others. It is the doctrines of the Incarnation and the Trinity that provide the linchpin of Christianity's understanding of the relation between God and the world, past, present, and future. They spell out what makes

Christianity, in Farmer's words, 'a theism of incarnation and reconciliation' that can still be held to surpass all other theistic world-views in its scope and power.

In the last chapter something was said about the evidence for incarnational belief. We now turn to its meaning and importance. I draw here especially on the work of Wolfhart Pannenberg[10] in systematic theology and the work of David Brown,[11] Thomas V. Morris,[12] and Richard Swinburne[13] in philosophical theology.

What does it mean to say that with Jesus Christ we have to do not simply with a supremely great teacher, prophet, and exemplar, but with God made man? It means that, for Christian understanding, the whole life and work of Jesus Christ were lived out from a centre in God. God, in person, is believed to have come to share our human lot, thereby showing us, in action and passion, the depths and extent of his love for humankind, and enabling men and women to be drawn, for ever, into the all-embracing life and love of the divine.

Clearly such an incarnation must have involved self-limitation, self-emptying, *kenosis*, on the part of God. (The reason why the divine subject of that human life has to be thought of as God the Son, not God *simpliciter,* will be made clear shortly when we turn to the doctrine of the Trinity.) For incarnation to be real, the human vehicle of the divine life had to be a genuine human being—in fact, as pointed out in Chapter 4, a Jew, nurtured in the faith of Israel. This self-emptying must have entailed limitation in knowledge and power, compatible with Jesus being a first-century Palestinian Jew. The man Jesus, we may well suppose (*pace* Michael Dummett), could not, as such, have known that he was God the Son incarnate. But such a kenotic Christology is pressed too far if it is held to involve the abandonment of the divine attributes of omnipotence and omniscience by God the Son. The divine subject of the incarnate life must have remained aware of what he was doing in taking our nature upon him and living a human life on Earth.

This means that we have to distinguish between two subjectivities where God incarnate is concerned. *Qua* God, he retained the divine attributes and powers. *Qua* man, he was limited to a first-century Jewish viewpoint. Such a 'two consciousnesses' view of the Incarnation has been argued for, in detail, by T. V. Morris. According to Morris's analysis, the divine mind of God the Son has to be thought of as containing the human mind of Jesus without being contained by it. But the logic of God incarnate requires much more than this. Morris insists, quite rightly, that God the Son has to be acknowledged as the ultimate subject of Jesus' thought and action, even if Jesus, *qua* man, was aware of no more than a profound love of, and communion with, God and a unique vocation and insight. In other words, the human subject has to be distinguished from the divine subject, even when the former was the incarnate form of the latter.

To develop this view a little further: the incarnate one, *qua* man, was not omnipotent. But it was the omnipotence of God the Son that included the power to channel his divine personhood through the humanity of Jesus, and it was the divine omnipotence that manifested itself humanly in Jesus' healing powers and in what he made of his Jewish inheritance. Presumably, too, it was his being God incarnate that ensured his sinlessness. Similarly, Jesus himself was not omniscient; but the omniscience of God the Son included knowing what it was like to be one of us. And it was the divine omniscience that manifested itself humanly in Jesus' knowing both the secrets of the human heart and the reconciling power of God's love.

In the last chapter I mentioned some of the reasons given by Swinburne as to why the theist might expect an incarnation of God. Similarly, the scope of Christian incarnational theology can be shown if we attempt to spell out what would be lost to a total Christian world-view should the doctrine of the Incarnation be demythologized.[14] This may sound a somewhat negative approach, but in fact it involves the highly positive task of bringing out the illuminating and existential power of the doctrine in question. That is to say, by explicating the rationale of incarnational theology, one shows not only its logic and metaphysics, as Morris does, but also its fruitfulness for both theological understanding and Christian life. This can be shown in at least five ways: first, in terms of what it means to encounter the love of God in person; secondly, in terms of what the Incarnation reveals about the true nature of humanity; thirdly, in terms of what it reveals about the mutuality, in God, of love given and love received; fourthly, in terms of what has actually been done to bring about forgiveness and reconciliation with God; and fifthly, in terms of what has been revealed, through Christ's Resurrection, about the future consummation of the whole creative process, when God will be all in all.

Let us explore each of these five aspects of the Incarnation's rationale a little further. The last three will bring us to the other main areas of Christian doctrine singled out above: trinitarian theology, soteriology, and eschatology. We shall find that none of these can be considered apart from the Incarnation.

Of course, men and women of faith in every theistic religion encounter God's love, God's command, God's call, God's inspiration, and God's succour personally, in ways that bear fruit in the lives of mystics, saints, and prophets, and in many, less dramatic, graced and holy lives. But where God comes to meet us in person, at our own level, in and as one of us, a different and more profound mode of personal encounter with the divine is made possible and real. Those who see God in Jesus Christ, at that time face to face, and ever since, sacramentally and in Christian prayer, are given something new and something that is definitive for the whole future of the Creator–creature relation. The implications of this for knowledge and experience of God as triune—indeed, for humanity's being taken into the triune life of God—will be spelled out shortly.

But before we address those points, it is worth pausing to consider the way in which God incarnate, in and as one of us, reveals the true essence of humanity. The life of Jesus is an icon not only of divinity but also of what it is to be a human being. We see this in Jesus, the man for others, as Karl Barth has memorably shown, in contrasting Jesus with the philosopher Friedrich Nietzsche's *Übermensch* ('Superman'),[15] and we see it, above all, in Jesus' relation to his heavenly Father. It is in such a relation that true humanity is seen to lie. Christian humanism is not a matter of trying to copy the life of Jesus. His vocation was unique, and his form of life—that of a wandering, celibate, Jewish rabbi—was but one of many possible forms of human existence, including the married state, that of the artist or the scientific genius, or whatever. A human life necessarily has a limited, particular form, exclusive of innumerable others. That goes for God incarnate as for any other human being. The perfection and paradigmatic nature of Jesus' life and work are revealed in the way in which, from within the chosen parameters of his vocation and his life story,

Jesus lived a life of unclouded openness to the Father's will and love.

We turn now to consider the logic, scope, and power of that second focal Christian doctrine, the doctrine of the Trinity. In doing so, we do not, of course, turn aside from the rationale of incarnational theology. For it was undoubtedly belief in the divinity of Christ that led to the development of an internally differentiated concept of God. Sense had to be made of the idea that a man who prayed to, and was in loving communion with, his heavenly Father, was himself God made man. This was seen as best modelled on a son–father relation. Equally, it was the gift of the Spirit and experience of the Spirit in the believer's heart, interceding 'with sighs too deep for words' (Rom. 8: 26), that led to the development of a threefold rather than a dual conception of that inner differentiation in God. As David Brown argues,[16] only a social model of the Trinity can account for these interpersonal relations within the deity. Only so can sense be made of the claim that God makes himself most fully known by coming amongst us in and as a man who prays to God, and in and as the Spirit who indwells the believer's heart and intercedes for us with the Father.

That there is also a purely a priori reason for a social trinitarian view of God is argued by Richard Swinburne.[17] He recovers and re-presents an independent argument, found in Richard of St Victor in the twelfth century,[18] whereby reflection on the very nature of love requires its prime analogate, the divine love, to be spelled out in terms of love given, love received, and love shared still more. The inadequacy of a concept of God modelled on an isolated individual becomes only too apparent. As mentioned at the beginning of this chapter, this is a major problem with the otherwise admirable comparative theology of Keith Ward.[19] In rejecting the social analogy for the doctrine of the Trinity, Ward is driven to suppose some creation or other to be necessary for God. Only by creating a world of persons could such a solitary God have an object for his love. Classical Christian trinitarianism, by contrast, sees relationality and mutual love as basic *within* the divine. The creation of a world of finite persons to love and be loved is not a necessity. It is a matter of pure grace.

That there are three personal centres in God, no less and no more, is also suggested by Richard of St Victor and Richard Swinburne on the basis of reflection on the nature of love. Certainly there must be love given and love received, at the very least, therefore, a bipolar relationality in God. But love's excellence has to go beyond any *egoisme à deux*. It has to involve love shared still more. For this is an essential aspect of what love means. Hence the postulation of three, not two, personal centres in God. But there are no comparable reasons, no further excellencies in the very nature of love, requiring us to postulate further differentiation, further personal centres or subjectivities in the divine.

The social analogy, whether derived from revelation and experience or from rational reflection, does not involve the postulation of three separate gods. That would be to think in terms of three finite, externally related deities. In the logic of the infinite, by contrast, the one, infinite, and absolute God is internally differentiated and interrelated. But, as Brown, Morris, and Swinburne show, that must mean three interrelated centres of consciousness and will in the divine.

The reason why Christians, like Jews and Muslims, still, for the most part, use the singular personal pronoun in speaking of, or praying to, God, is that it is God the Father whom they have in mind. Sometimes, of course, prayers are addressed to God the Son (the risen Christ) and sometimes, as at Pentecost, to God the Holy Spirit. But when Christians speak of, or pray to, the Holy and Blessed Trinity, three Persons in one God, then, clearly, plural personal pronouns are the order of the day.

Christianity's soteriology (its doctrine of salvation) has also received perceptive attention and analysis from philosophers of religion. I think particularly, in this connection, of two essays by Eleonore Stump[20] and another of Swinburne's books, *Responsibility and Atonement*.[21] Stump rightly places the emphasis on God's own self-sacrificial love in action, as the means whereby men and women are shown that they are forgiven, and opened up to transformation through the operations of divine grace. Swinburne, having offered powerful criticism of traditional atonement theory, has much light to throw on the subjects of forgiveness and reconciliation; but he is himself open to criticism for a somewhat strained insistence on reparation being an essential element in atonement.[22] While it is undoubtedly an important aspect of repentance for a person to make good, or to compensate for, the wrong he or she has done, sometimes this is just impossible; and, surely, forgiveness does not invariably depend on such reparation. It is more plausible to recognize that God's way, as revealed in the Incarnation, is the way of unconditional mercy and forgiveness. As Vernon White argues, in his *Atonement and Incarnation*,[23] it is the Incarnation that creates the conditions under which forgiven humanity can be renewed and taken into the triune life of God, through incorporation into Christ's risen Body.

The same point is made by John Lucas with his stress on identification as the keynote of atonement theory.[24] By identifying himself with humankind without reserve, God in Christ makes possible our reconciliation and our union with him. Eastern Orthodox talk of divinization, as, for example, in Athanasius's summary of the purpose of the Incarnation of the Word: 'He was made man that we might be made God',[25] is, admittedly, open to misunderstanding. It certainly does not mean that we lose our creaturely status. Rather, we are transformed by the gift of Christ's Spirit and enabled to share in that eternal filial relation to the Father, which is Christ's by nature.

In incarnational and trinitarian theology, therefore, we have to do with a world-view concerned not only with the present reality of things, but also with the forgiveness of sinful humanity and our transformation into conformity with God's intention for the ultimate future of creation.

Mention of the ultimate future brings us to the topic of Christian eschatology (the doctrine of the 'last things'). Here is another dimension of the Real, which is inaccessible to the natural and the human sciences. The curious discipline known as 'futurology' can only make tentative predictions, based on extrapolation from empirically known variables. Many of the relevant factors are unknown, and are themselves unpredictable, not least the scientific discoveries that made information technology possible, for example. The predictions of economists are notoriously fallible, like weather forecasts. The only sure prediction, long-term, from a scientific point of view, is the heat-death of the universe. (I do not think we can take seriously Frank Tipler's extravagant speculations about information technology creating a future cosmic 'mind'.[26] As argued in Chapter 1, such talk of computational 'mind' is at best metaphorical.) Philosophy too, by itself, cannot get us any further. It is notorious how even a thoroughly historicized metaphysics, such as Hegel's, culminates not in some eschatological future consummation but in the present, with philosophy's own conceptualization of Absolute Spirit. Christian eschatology, by contrast, in its many different forms, is based on revelation and experience: the teaching of Jesus about the Kingdom of God, the Easter story, and those existential moments of mystical or numinous experience which give a foretaste of eternity. All this forms the basis of the Church's developing doctrine concerning the consummation of all things. Examples of such theology include, most notably, the work of Teilhard de Chardin,[27] Jürgen Moltmann,[28] and the Process theologians,[29] although eschatology also plays a key, if more sober, role in the theology of Wolfhart Pannenberg.[30] I have surveyed and discussed all this material in my book *The Christian Hope*.[31]

No one denies the limitations of our understanding of these matters. The Christian tradition is quite clear that we see in a glass darkly (1 Cor. 13: 12), and that it is simply not given to us to know the precise nature of the final consummation of God's creative purposes in the end. But this whole dimension is at least opened up in Christian theology; and there are intimations and analogies that make the expression of the Christian hope a real possibility for participants in the experience, faith, and worship of the Church. This takes us way beyond anything that the natural or the human sciences can provide. Moreover, Christian theology can and does reflect rationally upon these otherwise unobtainable data and build the results into an overall, however tentative, world-view. The scope and force of this world-view, as briefly outlined here, contribute to the cumulative case for Christianity. And, as urged throughout this book, a developed, and rationally sifted, Christian theology both reinforces, and is reinforced by, the other elements in the cumulative case.

6

The Appeal to History III:
Universal History

THIS BOOK of Christian apologetic began, in Chapter 1, with a foray into natural theology, the teleological and axiological arguments sketched there being held to support a theistic world-view as offering the best explanation of those features of the world singled out for scrutiny. It was noted that, as we went on to consider the whole history of morality, culture, and religion, natural theology tended to shade into revealed theology. In Chapter 2, I argued that revealed theology is just as open to rational scrutiny and argumentation as is natural theology. Both contribute mutually reinforcing elements to the cumulative case for Christian belief. In Chapters 3 and 4 I insisted that the appeals to history which undoubtedly form an integral part of Christian apologetic have to be assessed in the light of the background evidence provided by the previous elements in the cumulative case. Moreover, the considerations sketched in Chapter 5 concerning the logic, scope, and power of developed Christian doctrine not only made their own contribution to the cumulative case, but also reinforced the appeals to history by offering the best explanation of the historical evidence surveyed in the previous two chapters.

Throughout I have emphasized the fact that these tentative, probabilistic arguments, open to discussion and assessment, if only hypothetically, by any reasonably sympathetic rational mind, do not constitute the epistemological foundation for Christian faith. At most, they provide support for a position occupied quite firmly by adherents of the Christian religion, whose faith and practice have their own internal warrant in terms of the basic belief structure of the Christian faith to which they are committed. The ontological foundation of Christian belief, if true, is of course the activity of God himself in creation, redemption, and sanctification. That activity is held by Christians to include God's acts in history, in the history of religions, in the history of Israel, in the Incarnation and the Resurrection, and in the work of the Spirit in and through the Christian Church and other channels of continuing revelation.

Experiential confirmation of all this plays an indispensable role *vis-à-vis* participation in the faith and practice of the Christian religion, as Austin Farrer insisted.[1] But it also plays an important role *vis-à-vis* the tentative, cumulative, apologetic case for Christian belief which we have been examining. Indeed, a further element in this apologetic is the fact that the alleged truth of Christianity offers the best explanation of the fact that for many people it does find experiential confirmation. But it only leads to confusion if we conflate these two roles. Best explanation arguments have at most a secondary function in relation to the vast majority of believers' own faith and experience.

So much by way of summary. In this final chapter I want to consider a further appeal to history that certainly has been made, and might still be made, in Christian apologetic: namely, the appeal to a providential reading of universal history as making most sense of the way in which world history has gone and is going. I do not add a reference to the future at this point, since the future does not yet supply *evidence* for the truth of Christian belief. Eschatological verification may in the end provide the clinching evidence, and appeal to it now may well play a role in showing the intelligibility and fact-asserting nature of Christian belief, as John Hick claims;[2] but it obviously cannot supply us with supporting evidence at the present time. What may be available, however, and what we might expect if Christianity is true, is some historical evidence that Christ is indeed the centre of history and that, in God's providence, just as the history of religions and the history of Israel can be seen, among other things, to have led up to the Incarnation, so the Christian centuries can be seen, among other things, to have borne marks of the special salvific efficacy of the Christ event.

Clearly, this is no easy task. World history, it might seem, is too various, too confused, too full of horrors, to bear out the supposition of its, even gradual, redemption since the time of Christ. It is a standard argument in Jewish apologetic to appeal to the evidently unredeemed nature of the world as evidence that the Messiah has not yet come. The rise of Islam six centuries after the Christ event, and its world-wide presence as a major factor in international relations today, make it very difficult to speak, in Hegelian terms, of universal history reaching a culminating phase either in Christianity or in Western philosophy. Moreover, the end of colonialism, the demise of Christendom, and the secularization of the Western world all make it hard to see the West as the spearhead and medium of the globalization of Christian values. Indeed, globalization in its more popular sense—that is to say, globalization of technology and trade, including globalization of information technology—appears to have nothing whatsoever to do with the risen Christ or the Kingdom of God. And what have theories of universal history to say about the emergence of China, one-third of humankind, as another major factor in the total world scene?

An immediate reaction would be to forswear theories of universal history, agree with Ranke or Butterfield that 'every epoch is immediate to God'[3] or that 'every generation is equidistant from eternity',[4] and appeal simply to the saints and to the Christian Church as evidence of the impact made in human history by the story of Jesus. Such appeals are indeed elements in the cumulative case for Christianity. Austin Farrer, in many of his sermons and papers, in addition to his stress on personal experiential verification of the divine providence, appealed to the public evidence of the lives of the saints who, as he put it, 'prove the real connection between religious symbols and everyday realities not by logical demonstration but by life', and who 'confute the logicians, not by logic, but by sanctity'.[5] One example, from the Middle Ages, is the figure of Julian of Norwich, who continues to capture the imagination and transform the lives of the many readers of her *Revelations of Divine Love*, the many visitors to the Julian Centre in Norwich, and the many members of Julian groups world-wide.[6] Other examples may be found in Trevor Beeson's *Rebels and Reformers*,[7] in which pen portraits are given of one hundred twentieth-century Christians, whose lives and work have borne astonishing witness to the power of Christ to challenge and transform not only the Church but secular society as well, not least in situations of tyranny and gross injustice. While Beeson's list contains some rather surprising names, the variety, range, and depth of these spiritual and theological paragons provide striking evidence for the efficacy, and perhaps the truth, of Christian belief. The same is true of the book edited by Helmut Gollwitzer and others, *Dying We Live*, in which the witness of Christian martyrs in Nazi Germany is most movingly displayed in letters written on the eve of execution.[8]

But individual Christians are nurtured in the Church, and it is on the Christian Church, the 'community of character', that Stanley Hauerwas and other communitarians focus when speaking of the redemptive effect of the Christ event.[9] Not that Hauerwas is interested in appealing to the fact of the Christian Church in human history as an element in a cumulative case for Christian belief. But an implication of his concentration on the Church as, despite its manifest faults, a foretaste of 'the peaceable kingdom',[10] is that we should not look elsewhere for evidence of the redemption of the world.

Hauerwas has, I think, successfully repudiated the charge of sectarianism.[11] For him, the Church is not an inward-looking school of the Christian virtues, which turns its back on the wicked world. Like Israel, its vocation is to show a better way, to be 'a light to the nations', and indeed, hopefully, to have some effect on the way in which the world's inherent violence may be tempered in spheres like that of the care of the retarded or the welcoming of strangers. But it is a leitmotif of Hauerwas's writings to oppose the association, let alone the identification, of the Kingdom with any social or political developments in the state or in the world. Thus, in his Gifford Lectures, *With the Grain of the Universe*,[12] Hauerwas develops his long-standing critique of Reinhold Niebuhr's Christian ethics as no more than a theological endorsement of American values: namely, liberality, democracy, and human rights. I shall return to these allegedly 'American' values shortly.

The title of Hauerwas's Gifford Lectures deserves some comment. It is taken from an essay by John Howard Yoder. Yoder wrote: 'The point that apocalyptic makes...is that people who bear crosses are working with the grain of the universe.'[13] The implication drawn from this by Yoder and Hauerwas is that it is the community of cross-bearers, the Church, not the world of the powerful, that manifests signs of the Kingdom. But if God's world does indeed have that grain, ought there not to be some evidence of that fact not only in the Church, not only in the tendency of the powerful, in the long run, and sometimes in the not so long run, to self-destruct, but also in the gradual penetration of society and the world by Kingdom values? And there is a further question to be put to Yoder and to Hauerwas: namely, whether the divine love that, despite appearances, gives the universe its grain has other aspects to it than simply that of crucifixion. Again, to this question I shall return.

I want now to contrast the view that it is only to the Church and to the saints that we should look, and appeal, for evidence of the redemption of the world with the view of a systematic theologian who encourages us to look for evidence in history of the wider and more universal sanctification of the world: namely, the Dutch theologian, Hendrikus Berkhof. In a number of books, especially *Christ the Meaning of History*,[14] and Chapters 52–5 of his one-volume dogmatics, *Christian Faith*,[15] Berkhof invites us to consider the renewing work of the Spirit of Christ crucified and risen not only in individual men and women of faith and in the Church that nurtures them, but also in the structures of society and in the world. While recognizing that only people can believe, repent, and mend their ways, he insists that there is an analogy between the sanctification of people and the sanctification of the world. Moreover, since the renewal of structures is not only the work of believers but to a large extent the work of people other than believers, we have to suppose that the Spirit works wherever the structures of society are remade to promote freedom and love. Admittedly, structures, as such, cannot be motivated, but they can be changed and renewed by the Spirit's acknowledged and unacknowledged work, through responsible believers and unbelievers alike. This leads Berkhof to consider the ways in which the Gospel, having entered the world, can be seen to have influenced cultures and structures both through and beyond the Church, whose Gospel it is. 'If there is something like a sanctification of societal structures,' writes Berkhof, 'it should be possible to illustrate that from the difference between those areas [where such influence has taken effect] and the rest of the world.'[16] We are reminded here of the point made in Chapter 4 about the differences in expectation made by differences in background evidence and background belief. Admittedly, Berkhof himself is diffident about talk of verification. He regards his reading of history as a faith statement, falsifiable perhaps, but not verifiable. We might wish to challenge this, as we did Plantinga's restriction of apologetic to negative apologetic. Berkhof's reason for diffidence regarding verifiability is the fact that the Spirit is not a datum of general experience. This is perfectly true. But the alleged effects of the Spirit's penetration are data of general experience, so there might well be a case for appeal to history in this connection after all.

The difference made by the Gospel's direct and indirect penetration is discernible, according to Berkhof, in the 1,300 years of European, now Western, cultural history. Increasingly, this has deviated from what he calls 'the universal human pattern' in the following respects. First came care of the sick and the poor, and rejection of the divine nature of the power of the state, and also the de-deification of nature. From Christianity came too an emphasis on labour and responsibility, and, over time, at least in principle, recognition of equality, and the ideal of social justice. 'In the long run', Berkhof goes on to say, 'democracy proves to be the societal form that is most suitable for the realisation of these ideas.'[17] Together with the notion of a goal-oriented history, this dynamic, emancipatory, and expansive cultural stream has had a strong impact on other parts of the world.

Berkhof is not afraid to speak of progress in this connection. I quote:

To mention only a few of these structural changes which have been product and factor [*sic*] in this process of development: equality before the law, the separation of the executive and judicial branches of the government, compulsory education, universal franchise, freedom of religion, communal care for the physically and mentally handicapped [here is one point where we note some commonality with Hauerwas] insurance, freedom of the press.[18]

But there are, of course, Berkhof says, limits and counter-trends, as we should expect, if the analogy holds with the struggle between the old and the new man in the believer. And further, this progress, especially in secularized form, is full of ambiguities that could lead to disaster. The biblical apocalyptic imagery portrays the possible intensification of conflict before the end.

Somewhere between Hauerwas and Berkhof stands Oliver O'Donovan, who, in *The Desire of the Nations*,[19] locates the rule of Christ first and foremost in the Church, but goes on to speak of the redemption of society, tracing the effect of the Christ event through Christendom and after Christendom in the restraint of secular power within the parameters of justice. He echoes, with some reservations about talk of 'Kingdom values', the views of Enda McDonagh in his book, *The Gracing of Society*, who writes of political theology being organized around the four 'Kingdom values' of justice, freedom, peace, and truth.[20] McDonagh is not himself concerned with appeals to history as evidence. But O'Donovan does write of freedom, mercy, natural right, and openness to free speech as aspects of liberal political order, whose historical development, to the extent that these 'values' are discernible in the structures and attitudes of society, 'bears the narrative of the Christ-event stamped upon it'.[21]

Of particular interest is O'Donovan's reply to a review article by Nicholas Wolterstorff in the *Scottish Journal of Theology*.[22] Against Wolterstorff's assertion that 'the inauguration of the church has changed nothing', O'Donovan insists that much has changed in history as a result of the Christ event and of the Church's involvement in history. But against Wolterstorff's 'Whiggish' view of inexorable progress through God's providence, irrespective of the Church, O'Donovan replies that there is nothing 'inexorable' about what he has claimed regarding the effect in history of the Christ event. Like Berkhof, he refers to apocalyptic's vision of the intensification of lawlessness as a parallel possibility and, we might think today, actuality. It is worth having before us for comparison two summary statements by Wolterstorff and O'Donovan. We note the very different understandings of providence that they invoke. Here is Wolterstorff: 'Slowly, episodically, but inexorably, the gross malformations of the state are being cured, so that it comes closer to doing what it's always been meant to do in God's providential order.'[23] And here is O'Donovan: 'political order is a *providential* ordering, not a created one, and so it has become diaphanous to the redeeming work of God taking on new forms in the light of the Christ-event.'[24]

Clearly for Wolterstorff, God's providence is an aspect of the order of creation, its effect being the inexorable cure of the state's malformations, while, for O'Donovan, God's providence works through the Christ event and its effects in Church and state, in ways which, as well as bringing about the partial redemption of society, can and do intensify the conflict between good and evil.

If we are tempted to side with Berkhof and O'Donovan against Hauerwas and to look for evidence in history for signs of the sanctification of the world, are we not in danger of falling foul of Hauerwas's critique of Niebuhr? Hauerwas, it will be recalled, accuses Niebuhr of attempting to provide a theological endorsement of American values. Are we not attempting a comparable endorsement of European values? Hauerwas, however, is most unfair to Niebuhr. Niebuhr himself was highly critical of Walter Rauschenbusch's and the Social Gospel's naïvety in thinking that the Kingdom of God could be, and in some areas had already been, realized on earth. Notoriously, Rauschenbusch went so far as to say that 'the larger part of the work of christianising our social order is already accomplished'.[25] It was a key element in Niebuhr's 'Christian realism' that whatever was achieved in the horizontal dimension of social and political reform was itself subject to criticism for its inadequacy from the vertical dimension of the divine love.[26]

In the second place, it is clear that Americans have no monopoly of concern for liberality, democracy, and human rights. Berkhof and O'Donovan show a much greater awareness of their historical origin in the Christian centuries, particularly in and from Europe and the West more generally. And their strength and appeal beyond Europe, although largely through European influence, is clear, not only from the pressures that made for their restitution in the countries of the former Soviet Union, with the churches playing a significant role in making that possible, as Pope John Paul II observed in his 1991 encyclical *Centesimus Annus*,[27] but also from their remarkable hold on at least the greater part of the Indian subcontinent, and elsewhere.

The view that the secularization of the European mind, to use the title of Owen Chadwick's book,[28] creates a problem for the view that Europe has a special role in the providential penetration of the world by 'Kingdom values' is easily countered, in the first place by recognition that secularization may itself be the condition of the wider dissemination of such values. The point is well articulated by Eberhard Jüngel: 'The Church may be thankful', he says, 'that its spiritual goods now exist in secular form. For example, the secular respect for freedom of conscience, the secular assertion of the inviolability of the dignity of the person, the secular commitment to protect handicapped human life, universal schooling and many other achievements of the modern constitutional state are secularised church treasures.'[29]

Secondly, it may be urged that European influence too, despite its largely Christian provenance, has no exclusive claim on the values in question. The social ethical implications of the Gospel find echoes in other philosophical and faith traditions, and what was said in Chapter 3 about 'other lights' can be drawn on to assist the case for recognition of the variety of resources for the humanization of the world. Moreover, the interaction between Christianity and other faiths works both ways. I have referred to Christianity's influence upon the development of Hindu social ethics. But that Christian theology and social ethics should themselves learn from other faiths is also clear. I mentioned in Chapter 4 examples given by David Brown of how Christians can learn from Judaism and Islam. Similarly, the Sri Lankan Jesuit, Aloysius Pieris, has urged, in his *An Asian Theology of Liberation*,[30] the need to learn from Buddhism in developing an indigenous liberation theology rather than just taking over a Western one. Similar points are made, in a more reformist vein, by the Japanese theologian Kosuke Koyama, about the Christian presence in the Far East.[31] Bishop C. F. Andrews in India used to say that he had learned more of what it meant to be a Christian from his Hindu friend, Mahatma Gandhi, than from many of his fellow Christians.[32]

Secularization is a highly ambiguous phenomenon. Despite what Jüngel said about giving thanks for the fact of secularized church treasures in Europe and elsewhere, the question remains how far they are sustainable without their Christian or religious framework. We recall again Elizabeth Anscombe's scepticism about the viability of the language of moral obligation divorced from its origin in theological ethics. And contemporary worries about the sustainability of the care of the retarded and the terminally ill in a purely secular culture suggest that secularized church treasures may cease to retain their hold on society's, and the medical profession's, imagination and commitment.

The theme of secularization may, however, have been over-stressed. In her book *Europe: The Exceptional Case*,[33] the sociologist Grace Davie argues that, on the world scene today, European secularization is the exception rather than the rule. In the United States, Latin America, and sub-Saharan Africa, to say nothing of the East and the Far East, modernization is far from being necessarily bound up with secularization.

The question still remains as to how far the values of freedom, mercy, natural right, and openness to free speech, to cite the O'Donovan quadrilateral again, stemming, as they largely do, from a Judaeo-Christian origin and transmitted, as they largely have been, through a European, Western culture, are potentially universal and global in their long-term impact.

Wolfhart Pannenberg has written interestingly about the way in which the movement towards European integration can play its role in pointing the way to a wider unification of the history of mankind. 'A united Europe', he says, 'will have to be able to display the humanity of its people in its culture and democratic structures in such a way that it exercises an attraction on the rest of mankind.'[34] To do so, Europe will need to recover its religious, Christian roots, and these too must achieve unification. The importance of the ecumenical movement and its quest for Christian unity was stressed by Pannenberg in his contribution to the Canterbury colloquium on *Christian Values in Europe* in 1993.[35] Interesting too is Pannenberg's defence of 'toleration' as a Christian virtue, despite the common view of tolerance as a product of the Enlightenment in reaction to the wars of religion: 'the divisions in the West', says Pannenberg,

opened the way to the thought of tolerance, not merely in civil life but also in the life and faith of the church. The church did not itself formulate this principle, though it would have been natural for it to do so. It reached it only by way of a detour *via* a world that was alienating itself from the church, and to this day divisions among Christians are making it take the lesson to heart even to the transforming of its relation to other religions.[36]

Something similar could be said about the abolition of slavery, about the abolition of capital punishment, and, more generally, about the values of restraint and the spirit of reconciliation that can come to colour social and political life in place of the vendetta mentality of ancient and, alas, some modern societies. The Truth and Reconciliation Commission in South Africa was a striking example of the way in which 'Kingdom values' could come to penetrate the life of a society in transition. Again, the question arises of how sustainable such social virtues are without their religious background. The same is true of the climate of trust of our fellow citizens and colleagues, of which Onora O'Neill spoke in her 2002 Reith Lectures.[37]

Lest this talk of 'Kingdom values' should appear to support the idea of restricting the European Community to countries with a Christian heritage, let it be said that the possibility, even the probability, of Turkey joining the Community is a welcome indication of the non-exclusive nature of these values.

Now I want to contrast the suggestion that there are discernible marks of the sanctification of the world in the partial implementation of these 'Kingdom values' in European and Western civilization and political order and their increasing world-wide impact, with a very different picture of the world scene coming from the Harvard Professor of International Relations, Samuel Huntington, in his much discussed book *The Clash of Civilizations.*[38]

The main theme of Huntington's book is that the end of the Cold War has resulted, not in the triumph of the West, to use the title of J. M. Roberts's 1985 book,[39] nor in the end of history, as Francis Fukayama suggested,[40] but in the emergence to positions of greater strength and influence of a number of civilizations, many, though not all, dominated by a core state, but each with a growing sense of ethnically or religiously reinforced identity. The risks to world peace from this new situation are no longer from intra-civilizational wars such as characterized European history for centuries, but from what Huntington calls fault-line wars between civilizations, as most obviously in the Balkans, Palestine, and Kashmir. He names nine such civilizations: Western (including Israel), Latin American, African, Islamic, Sinic, Hindu, Orthodox (including Russia, Serbia, and Greece), Buddhist, and Japanese. The emerging world scene is described with a wealth of detail and documentation, and the distribution of military power, economic muscle, and potentiality for modernization is graphically illustrated. Two leading motifs of the picture we are given are, first, the importance of religion as a resurgent factor in fostering civilizational identities, and, secondly, the rejection not only of Western military and economic supremacy, but also of Western culture—at any rate, Western culture as seen by non-Western eyes. In a way, this reinforces and extends Grace Davie's point: for other civilizations, modernization not only does not involve secularization, it does not necessarily mean Westernization. As Huntington sums up, 'in fundamental ways, the world is becoming more modern and less Western.'[41]

The Western culture rejected, by the Chinese and by the Muslim world, for example, has little to do with the 'Kingdom values' singled out in the present chapter as marks of the redemption of society. What other people see, from the media as much as from experience of victimization, is a rampantly individualistic, egoistic culture, overwhelmed by consumerism, to say nothing of crime and drugs. But, as Huntington points out, even the values of democracy and human rights, which are held by Christian social ethicists such as Niebuhr, John C. Bennett,[42] and Hendrikus Berkhof to embody Christian principles and to be in themselves universalizable, are increasingly held, in many non-Christian civilizations, to reflect purely Western dominance of international institutions. I shall return to this point shortly.

Huntington speaks of Christianity as the religion of the West; but he does not take note of the fact that four of his nine civilizations—Latin American, Orthodox, and African (sub-Saharan, of course, the north belonging largely to the Muslim world), as well as the Western—are informed by Christianity, with Latin America and Africa being its most evident growing points. He ignores the ancient Christian presence in Egypt, Ethiopia, and South India, the extraordinary resilience of the tiny Christian communities in China, and, above all, the international and intercivilizational range of the Roman Catholic Church and the World Council of Churches. These latter have their faults, as Ronald Preston makes clear in his book *Confusions in Christian Social Ethics: Problems for Geneva and Rome*,[43] but there remains a solid body of social ethical teaching, of universal scope, coming from Vatican II and the papal encyclicals, and, of a more radical nature, from the General Assemblies of the World Council of Churches. One thinks not only of such teaching, but of its embodiment in the Christian communities of which the communitarians make so much, as well as in countless individual Christians from the Middle East, the East, and the Far East, as well as from the Christian civilizations themselves. Moreover, criticism of individualism, egoism, consumerism, and the negative side of Western 'culture' comes as much from Christian sources as from elsewhere.

So Huntington's conception of Christianity as the motivating ideology in the identity of the West is very inadequate. But so too is his conception of Islam. There is no doubt about the way in which Islam, especially Islamic fundamentalism, can and does motivate ethnic and civilizational identity, and foment anti-Western attitudes, but there is much else to say about the core values of Islam, as evidenced in the history of its golden age in Spain, in its fostering of familial and communal, as well as ethical and aesthetic, forms of life and social practice. The understanding of Islam and of the possibilities of creative interrelationship between Islam and Christianity to be found in the writings of Montgomery Watt,[44] Wilfred Cantwell Smith,[45] and Kenneth Cragg,[46] for example, is nowhere mentioned in Huntington's work.

But what of democracy and human rights? Huntington is quite correct in pointing out that the recovery or establishment of democratic political systems in the 1970s and 1980s took place in countries where Christian and Western influences were strong. It is also the case that, in the period since the end of the Cold War, American commitment to the promotion and consolidation of democracy has met with little success—indeed, with marked resistance—in Asia and the Middle East, especially where Islam predominates. In fact, the more democracy is identified with America and the West, and the greater the resurgence of other civilizations hostile to the West, the more resistance there is likely to be. Non-Westerners are very wary of Western, especially American, double standards where democracy is concerned. Western countries were generally glad when the Algerian military intervened to prevent the democratic election of a fundamentalist Islamic government there. And the West is notorious for its support of friendly non-democratic countries such as Saudi Arabia.

Huntington says nothing about Indian democracy, and little about the impact of the democratic election of a President in Iran, despite real power in that country remaining with the mullahs. But the lesson to be drawn from the tendency to identify democracy with the West, is not, I suggest, a Hauerwasian withdrawal of Christian social ethics from an interest in democracy, but recognition of the need to detach the ethics of democracy from monopolization, and indeed corruption, by the West. The considerations that led both Niebuhr and Berkhof to see in democratic institutions the best framework for the realization of 'Kingdom values', despite their Western origin, may well, in the long run, make themselves felt more powerfully in non-Western contexts. And anyone who sees these values as reflecting the grain of the universe, if I may borrow or steal that notion from Yoder and Hauerwas, is going to expect the eventual spread of democratic forms of political order.

Much the same may be said of human rights. Huntington observes a comparable tendency in Asian and Islamic contexts to see the 1948 United Nations Universal Declaration on Human Rights as the product of Western dominance and influence after the Second World War. Resistance to the promotion of human rights, as understood in the USA and the West, was only too clear at the UN World Conference on Human Rights in Vienna in 1993, where only a much weaker declaration was possible in face of a majority of non-Western nations' insistence on respect for state sovereignty. Huntington quotes one Asian critic of the West: 'For the first time since the Universal Declaration was adopted in 1948, countries not thoroughly steeped in the Judaeo-Christian and natural law traditions are in the first rank. That unprecedented situation will define the new international politics of human rights. It will also multiply the occasions for conflict.'[47]

This may well be so in the immediate and short-term future. But in the long run, the ideas underlying not only the Universal Declaration but also the International Court and the War Crimes Tribunal in The Hague are not going to go away. The transcendence of state sovereignty institutionalized in this latter body finds resistance at present, not only in many Asian and Muslim countries, but also in Orthodox countries and indeed in the USA. Yet the pressures that led Serbia to send Milošević to The Hague were not solely economic. And the conceptions of justice and human rights at issue are no more the monopoly of the West than the conception of democracy. The protesters in Tiananmen Square may have been crushed, but in the long run, as the saying goes, 'truth will out', as happened against all pragmatic expectation in the Soviet Union and in South Africa.

Rights talk, like democracy, can be abused. It needs to be complemented by talk of responsibility. This was another of Onora O'Neill's themes in her 2002 Reith Lectures; and it was very much the theme of the Chicago Declaration of the 1993 Parliament of World Religions, *Toward a Global Ethic*,[48] drafted by Hans Küng. This thoroughly inter-faith declaration, signed by representatives of all the world religions, including Islam, may be favourably contrasted with the UN Vienna Declaration of the same year and held to be more in accord with the grain of the universe than that 'flawed and contradictory' document, as it has been called by one human rights supporter at the Vienna Conference.[49] The basic principle underlying the Chicago Declaration was the golden rule: do as you would be done by, versions of which are to be found in every major religion. From this the Declaration derived four irrevocable directions for ordering human behaviour: commitment to a culture of non-violence and respect for human life, commitment to a culture of solidarity and a just economic order, commitment to a culture of tolerance and a life of truthfulness, and commitment to a culture of equal rights and partnership between men and women. We may well be reminded on reading this of Enda McDonagh's four basic 'Kingdom values' and of what I called the O'Donovan quadrilateral. Incidentally, the one issue on which the UN Vienna Conference did make progress was women's rights, strongly endorsed there by the non-Western majority, as they were in Chicago by all the religions, including Islam.

The detachment of the ethics of democracy and human rights from their Western context and origin can itself be read in providential terms. Karl Barth once said to an audience of foreign students in Basel: 'The day may come when [essential Christianity] will be better understood and better lived in Asia and Africa than in our old Europe.'[50] The same may well be true of the 'Kingdom values' under discussion here.

A topic stressed by all the Christian ethicists considered in this chapter, by Hauerwas as well as by Berkhof and O'Donovan, is the welcoming of strangers. Huntington, in his Kissinger-like style of *Realpolitik*, has a painful section on immigration, showing, in detail, how Western governments, in Europe and the USA, have all found themselves driven to impose severe limits on the numbers of immigrants and asylum seekers that they are now willing to accept.[51] And we are only too aware of how extreme right-wing parties in France, the Netherlands, Germany, and Italy, and to a degree in Britain too, have benefited from, as well as cultivated, the increasing public concern over loss of national and cultural identity through the sheer number of, especially, non-Western immigrants.

This subject was raised by O'Donovan in the course of his reply to Wolterstorff's assertion that the proclamation of Christ's Kingship makes no difference to the way in which such issues are handled politically.[52] O'Donovan is acutely aware of the paradox created by recognition both that governments have a right to ensure that immigration is kept to a sustainable level and also that potential immigrants have a right to be treated fairly and justly. But the ethics of the Kingdom do make a difference in theory, and have made a difference in practice. Governments cannot get away with defending their people's identities irrespective of considerations of justice.

The penultimate section of Huntington's book consists of a terrifying sketch of possible circumstances that might lead, in the course of the twenty-first century, to a major fault-line war between an emerging Chinese civilization and the West. But I want to draw attention to the surprising final, brief, section of Huntington's book, where he offers advice on how to avoid such major fault-line clashes between civilizations.[53] The requirements of peace in a multi-civilizational world, he suggests, are threefold: first, that core states should refrain from intervening in conflicts in other civilizations; second, that such conflicts should be contained or halted through joint mediation between core states; and third, and most intriguingly from our present point of view, what he calls 'the commonalities rule': peoples of all civilizations should search for and attempt to expand the values, institutions, and practices they have in common with peoples of other civilizations.[54] At this point Huntington sounds remarkably like Hans Küng, in the latter's efforts, as at the World Parliament of Religions, to promote a global ethic.[55] Indeed, Huntington refers explicitly to the fact that the major religions of the world also share key values in common; and he praises Michael Walzer's work on the 'thin', minimalist, but common morality to be found in all the 'thick', diverse moralities of the world religions and civilizations.[56]

There is a curious contradiction here between the view we find in the greater part of Huntington's book, that religion is the motivating force of divergent ethnicities and civilizational identities, and the view now expressed that the religions foster the key common values necessary for world peace. It is not easy to know how serious he is about the latter view. On one page he says: 'In a multicivilizational world, the constructive course is to renounce universalism, accept diversity, and seek commonalities.'[57] Two pages later, he says: 'if humans are ever to develop a universal civilization, it will emerge gradually through the exploration and expansion of these commonalities.'[58] This ambiguity regarding universalism reflects the lack of serious investigation of the key values in question, to say nothing of the universal import of some, at any rate, of the 'thick' values given to the world by particular histories, religions, and cultures.

I am not deterred, therefore, by *The Clash of Civilizations* from looking for, and appealing to, signs or marks in the history of the world of its penetration by the Gospel. Certainly we have learned to appreciate diversity in God's providential ordering of things, as Robert Adams has urged. Certainly we look for analogies and parables of the Kingdom in other faith traditions, as even Karl Barth allowed. But that there is evidence, in the gradual, episodic, though hardly 'inexorable', transformations of public consciousness and political order, not only in Christendom, but after Christendom, of the sanctification of the world seems arguable and, at best, quite plausible. So, I suggest, there are further appeals to history to be added to the cumulative case for Christian belief. In addition to natural theology and the inner rationale of Christian doctrine, in addition to the history of morality and religion, in addition to the faith of Israel and the story of Jesus, not least his Resurrection, in addition to the lives of the saints and the Christian Church, in so far as it actually does embody and manifest the fruits of the Spirit, the apologist will also appeal to the ways in which the values of the Kingdom can be seen to have penetrated society and made their contribution to the redemption of the world.

Notes

CHAPTER 1   A CASE FOR THEISM

1. See James Wm. McClendon, Jr., and James M. Smith, *Understanding Religious Convictions* (Notre Dame, Ind.: University of Notre Dame Press, 1975).
2. P. F. Strawson, *Individuals: An Essay in Descriptive Metaphysics* (London: Methuen & Co. Ltd., 1959).
3. Michael Dummett, *The Logical Basis of Metaphysics* (London: Duckworth, 1991), ch. 15. The view that Dummett is a constructivist in all areas of philosophy is surely mistaken.
4. J. L. Austin, *Philosophical Papers* (Oxford: Clarendon Press, 1961), ch. 7.
5. Ian G. Barbour, *Religion in an Age of Science* (London: SCM Press, 1990).
6. John D. Barrow, *Theories of Everything: The Quest for Ultimate Explanation* (Oxford: Oxford University Press, 1990).
7. John C. Eccles, *The Human Mystery* (New York: Springer International, 1979).
8. Arthur Peacocke, *Theology for a Scientific Age* (Oxford: Basil Blackwell, 1990).
9. John Polkinghorne, *Science and Christian Belief* (London: SPCK, 1994).

10. Peter Geach, *God and the Soul* (London: Routledge & Kegan Paul, 1969), 41.

11. John R. Searle, *The Mystery of Consciousness* (London: Granta Publications, 1997). See also his *Minds, Brains and Science* (London: BBC, 1984), and *The Rediscovery of the Mind* (Cambridge, Mass.: MIT Press, 1992).

12. Anthony Kenny, *The Metaphysics of Mind* (Oxford: Clarendon Press, 1989). On the inadequacies of evolutionary naturalism in respect of giving an account of human rationality, see also Thomas Nagel, *The Last Word* (New York: Oxford University Press, 1997).

13. H. D. Lewis, *The Elusive Mind* (London: George Allen & Unwin, 1969).

14. Richard Swinburne, *The Evolution of the Soul* (Oxford: Clarendon Press, 1986).

15. Karl R. Popper and John C. Eccles, *The Self and its Brain: An Argument for Interactionism* (New York: Springer International, 1977).

16. Bertrand Russell, *History of Western Philosophy* (London: George Allen & Unwin, 1946), ch. 13.

17. Alvin Plantinga, 'Advice to Christian Philosophers', *Faith and Philosophy* 1 (1984), 253–71.

18. Derek Parfit, *Reasons and Persons* (Oxford: Oxford University Press, 1986).

19. David Hume, *A Treatise of Human Nature, Book I: Of the Understanding* (London: John Noon, 1739), part IV, section vi.

20. Norman Kemp Smith (trans.), *Immanuel Kant's Critique of Pure Reason* (London: Macmillan, 2nd impression, 1933), 152 ff.

21. John Macmurray, *The Self as Agent* (London: Faber & Faber, 1957), and *Persons in Relation* (London: Faber & Faber, 1961).

22. Swinburne, *Evolution of the Soul*, ch. 10.

23. Karl R. Popper, *Objective Knowledge: An Evolutionary Approach* (Oxford: Clarendon Press, 1972), ch. 3.

24. Roger Penrose, *Shadows of the Mind* (Oxford: Oxford University Press, 1994), part II, 8.7.
25. John D. Barrow and Frank J. Tipler, *The Anthropic Cosmological Principle* (Oxford: Clarendon Press, 1986), ch. 6.
26. Ibid. ch. 9.
27. Pierre Teilhard de Chardin, *The Phenomenon of Man* (London: William Collins & Co., 1959), book 3.
28. Austin Farrer, *The Freedom of the Will* (London: Adam & Charles Black, 1958).
29. J. R. Lucas, *The Freedom of the Will* (Oxford: Clarendon Press, 1970).
30. In an obituary of Elizabeth Anscombe, *The Tablet*, 13 January 2001.
31. C. S. Lewis, *Miracles*, rev. edn. (London: Collins, 1960), ch. 3.
32. Elizabeth Anscombe, 'Causality and Determination', in *Metaphysics and the Philosophy of Mind: Collected Philosophical Papers, ii* (Oxford: Basil Blackwell, 1981), 145 f.
33. Stephen Clark, *God, Religion and Reality* (London: SPCK, 1998), 96–101.
34. Anscombe, 'Causality and Determination', 146.
35. On the postulates of practical reason, see Immanuel Kant, *The Critique of Practical Reason* (1788), book II, ch. II, sect. VI.
36. Allen W. Wood, *Kant's Moral Religion* (Ithaca, NY: Cornell University Press, 1970).
37. Iris Murdoch, *Metaphysics as a Guide to Morals* (London: Chatto & Windus, 1992).
38. Ibid. 508.
39. Don Cupitt, *The Religion of Being* (London: SCM Press, 1998).
40. D. M. MacKinnon, *The Problem of Metaphysics* (Cambridge: Cambridge University Press, 1974).
41. Ibid. 147.
42. Ibid. 145.

43. J. L. Mackie, *Ethics: Inventing Right and Wrong* (Harmondsworth: Penguin Books, 1977).

44. Brian Hebblethwaite, *The Ocean of Truth: A Defence of Objective Theism* (Cambridge: Cambridge University Press, 1988), ch. 7.

45. Peter L. Berger, *A Rumour of Angels: Modern Society and the Rediscovery of the Supernatural* (Harmondsworth: Penguin Books, 1971), 76–9.

46. Bernard Levin, *Enthusiasms* (London: Jonathan Cape, 1983), 158.

47. See T. M. Knox (trans.), *Hegel's Aesthetics* (Oxford: Clarendon Press, 1975).

48. R. G. Collingwood, *Speculum Mentis* (Oxford: Clarendon Press, 1924), ch. 3.

49. George Steiner, *Real Presences: Is There Anything* In *What We Say?* (London: Faber & Faber, 1989).

50. Ibid. 226 f.

51. Brian Hebblethwaite, *The Essence of Christianity: A Fresh Look at the Nicene Creed* (London: SPCK, 1996), 26.

52. T. S. Eliot, *On Poetry and Poets* (London: Faber & Faber, 1957), 207–27.

53. T. S. Eliot, *Selected Essays* (London: Faber & Faber, 1932), 237–77.

54. George Steiner, *On Difficulty and Other Essays* (New York: Oxford University Press, 1978), ch. 7.

55. Ralph Cudworth, *The True Intellectual System of the Universe* (1678).

56. Douglas Hedley, *Coleridge, Philosophy and Religion* (Cambridge: Cambridge University Press, 2000).

57. Ibid. 23.

58. See Penrose, *Shadows of the Mind.*

59. See Ray Monk, *Bertrand Russell 1921–70: The Ghost of Madness* (London: Jonathan Cape, 2000), 267–70.

60. See Clark, *God, Religion and Reality.*

61. See the relevant volumes of the *Cambridge Companion* series, published by Cambridge University Press: *Descartes*, ed. John Cottingham (1986); *Malebranche*, ed. Steven Nadler (2000); *Leibniz*, ed. Nicholas Jolley (1995); *Spinoza*, ed. Don Garrett (1996).

62. Charles Taylor, *Hegel* (Cambridge: Cambridge University Press, 1975).

63. Peter C. Hodgson, 'Georg Wilhelm Friedrich Hegel', in Ninian Smart *et al.* (eds.), *Nineteenth-Century Religious Thought in the West*, i (Cambridge: Cambridge University Press, 1985), 81–121.

64. Raymond Plant, *Hegel* (London: Phoenix, 1997).

65. J. R. Illingworth, *Personality, Human and Divine* (London: Macmillan, 1894).

66. Hastings Rashdall, *Philosophy and Religion* (London: Duckworth, 1924).

67. C. C. J. Webb, *God and Personality* (London: George Allen & Unwin, 1919).

68. A. E. Taylor, 'Theism', in *Hastings Encyclopaedia of Religion and Ethics*, xii (Edinburgh: T. & T. Clark, 1921), 261–87.

69. William Temple, *Nature, Man and God* (London: Macmillan, 1934).

70. See A. N. Whitehead, *Process and Reality* (New York: Macmillan, 1929).

71. On the later Heidegger, see George Pattison, *The Later Heidegger* (London: Routledge, 2000).

72. Ninian Smart, *World Philosophies* (London: Routledge, 1999).

73. Eliot Deutsch and Ron Bontekoe (eds.), *A Companion to World Philosophies* (Oxford: Blackwell, 1997).

74. Julius Lipner, *The Face of Truth: A Study of Meaning and Metaphysics in the Vedantic Theology of Ramanuja* (London: Macmillan, 1986).

75. R. C. Zaehner, *Evolution in Religion: A Study in Sri Aurobindo and Pierre Teilhard de Chardin* (Oxford: Clarendon Press, 1971).

76. Keith Ward, *Religion and Revelation* (Oxford: Clarendon Press, 1994); *idem, Religion and Creation* (Oxford: Clarendon Press, 1996); *idem, Religion and Human Nature* (Oxford: Clarendon Press, 1998); *idem, Religion and Community* (Oxford: Clarendon Press, 2000).

77. See Christopher Menzel, 'Theism, Platonism and the Metaphysics of Mathematics', *Faith and Philosophy* 4 (1987), 365–82.

78. e.g. Rudolf Otto, *The Idea of the Holy*, Eng. trans. (Oxford: Oxford University Press, 1923).

79. e.g. Gerardus van der Leeuw, *Religion in Essence and Manifestation: A Study in Phenomenology* (London: George Allen & Unwin, 1938).

80. e.g. Ninian Smart, *Dimensions of the Sacred: An Anatomy of the World's Beliefs* (London: Harper Collins, 1996).

81. e.g. Ernst Troeltsch, *Religion in History: Essays Translated by James Luther Adams* (Edinburgh: T. & T. Clark, 1991).

82. e.g. Mircea Eliade, *A History of Religious Ideas*, 3 vols. (Chicago: University of Chicago Press, 1978–85).

CHAPTER 2   THE RATIONALITY OF REVELATION

1. Joseph Butler, *The Analogy of Religion Natural and Revealed to the Constitution and Course of Nature* (first published, London, 1736). The edition used here is J. H. Bernard (ed.), *The Works of Bishop Butler*, ii (London: Macmillan, 1900).

2. John Henry Newman, *An Essay in Aid of a Grammar of Assent* (London: Burns, Oates, 1870), chs. 9 and 10.

3. F. R. Tennant, *Philosophical Theology*, ii (Cambridge: Cambridge University Press, 1930), chs. 3 and 4.

4. Basil Mitchell, *The Justification of Religious Belief* (London: Macmillan, 1973).

5. Richard Swinburne, *The Existence of God* (Oxford: Clarendon Press, 1979; rev. edn. 1991).

6. Robert Prevost, *Probability and Theistic Explanation* (Oxford: Clarendon Press, 1990).

7. William J. Abraham, 'Cumulative Case Arguments for Christian Theism', in W. J. Abraham and Steven W. Holtzer (eds.), *The Rationality of Religious Belief: Essays in Honour of Basil Mitchell* (Oxford: Clarendon Press, 1987), 17–37.

8. Thomas Aquinas, *Summa Theologiae*, 1a.1.2 *responsio*, and 1a.2.2 *ad* 1.

9. Austin Farrer, 'Very God and Very Man', in Austin Farrer, *Interpretation and Belief* (London: SPCK, 1976), 128.

10. Tennant, *Philosophical Theology*, ii. 79.

11. *St. Anselm: Basic Writings*, trans. S. N. Deane (La Salle, Ill.: Open Court Publishing Company, 1961), 1–34.

12. Karl Barth, *Anselm: Fides Quaerens Intellectum*, Eng. trans. (London: SCM Press, 1960).

13. Alvin Plantinga, *God, Freedom and Evil* (London: George Allen & Unwin, 1974).

14. Keith Ward, *Rational Theology and the Creativity of God* (Oxford: Basil Blackwell, 1982).

15. *St. Anselm: Basic Writings*, 177.

16. Butler, *Analogy of Religion*, 164 (Part II, ch. 3, para. 1).

17. Ibid. 221 (Part II, ch. 7, para. 2).

18. Ibid. 255 (Part II, ch. 7, para. 45).

19. H. H. Farmer, *Revelation and Religion: Studies in the Theological Interpretation of Religious Types* (London: Nisbet & Co., 1954). This was the first series of Farmer's Gifford Lectures (delivered in 1950). He was unwilling to publish the second series (delivered in 1951); but now, nearly fifty years later, the second series has been published under the title *Reconciliation and Religion: Some Aspects of the Uniqueness of Christianity as a Reconciling Faith*, ed. and introduced by C. H. Partridge (Lewiston, NY: The Edwin Mellen Press, 1998).

20. Francis Bacon, *De Dignitate et Augmentis Scientiarum* (1623), iii. 2.
21. Farmer, *Revelation and Religion*, 18.
22. Ibid. 19.
23. James Barr, *Biblical Faith and Natural Theology* (Oxford: Clarendon Press, 1993).
24. James Barr, *The Concept of Biblical Theology: An Old Testament Perspective* (London: SCM Press, 1999).
25. Ibid. 479.
26. Ibid. 490.
27. Ibid. 495.
28. Terence Penelhum, *Reason and Religious Faith* (Oxford: Westview Press, 1995), ch. 5.
29. Alvin Plantinga, *Warranted Christian Belief* (New York: Oxford University Press, 2000), 477.
30. Ibid. 342–9.
31. Alvin Plantinga, 'Christian Philosophy at the End of the 20th Century', in James F. Sennett (ed.), *The Analytic Theist: An Alvin Plantinga Reader* (Grand Rapids, Mich.: William B. Eerdmans, 1998), 328–52.
32. See Ch. 1, n. 1.
33. William Alston, *Perceiving God: The Epistemology of Religious Experience* (Ithaca, NY: Cornell University Press, 1991).
34. Richard Swinburne, *The Existence of God*, rev. edn. (Oxford: Clarendon Press, 1991), Appendix A.
35. Martin Rees, *Just Six Numbers* (London: Weidenfeld & Nicolson, 1999), ch. 11.
36. Plantinga, *Warranted Christian Belief*, 374.
37. Andrew Moore, 'Philosophy of Religion or Philosophical Theology?', *International Journal of Systematic Theology* 3 (2001), 309–328.
38. Ibid. 310.

39. Donald MacKinnon, *Explorations in Theology*, V (London: SCM Press, 1979), 89.
40. Richard Swinburne, *The Coherence of Theism* (Oxford: Clarendon Press, 1977; rev. edn. 1993).
41. Richard Swinburne, *The Existence of God* (Oxford: Clarendon Press, 1979; rev. edn. 1991).
42. Richard Swinburne, *Faith and Reason* (Oxford: Clarendon Press, 1981).
43. Richard Swinburne, *Responsibility and Atonement* (Oxford: Clarendon Press, 1989).
44. Richard Swinburne, *Revelation: From Metaphor to Analogy* (Oxford: Clarendon Press, 1992).
45. Richard Swinburne, *The Christian God* (Oxford: Clarendon Press, 1994).
46. Richard Swinburne, *Providence and the Problem of Evil* (Oxford: Clarendon Press, 1998).
47. Donald MacKinnon, *The Problem of Metaphysics* (Cambridge: Cambridge University Press, 1974).
48. Donald MacKinnon, *Themes in Theology: The Three-Fold Cord: Essays in Philosophy, Politics and Theology* (Edinburgh: T. & T. Clark, 1987), 145–67.
49. See e.g. Thomas V. Morris, *The Logic of God Incarnate* (Notre Dame, Ind.: University of Notre Dame Press, 1986).
50. See e.g. van Inwagen's articles on 'Incarnation and Christology' and 'Trinity' in the *Routledge Encyclopedia of Philosophy* (London: Routledge, 1998), iv. 725–32, ix. 457–61.
51. Plantinga, 'Christian Philosophy', 341.
52. Moore, 'Philosophy of Religion', 312.
53. Brian Hebblethwaite, 'God and Truth', *Kerygma und Dogma* 40 (1944), 10.
54. Moore, 'Philosophy of Religion', 317.
55. Alasdair MacIntyre, *Whose Justice? Which Rationality?* (London: Gerald Duckworth & Co., 1988).

56. Kelvin Knight (ed.), *The MacIntyre Reader* (Notre Dame, Ind.: University of Notre Dame Press, 1998), 152.

57. Norman Kemp Smith (trans.), *Immanuel Kant's Critique of Pure Reason* (London: Macmillan, 2nd impression 1933), 635.

58. James Creed Meredith (trans.), *Kant's Critique of Judgement* (Oxford: Clarendon Press, 1952).

59. Newman, *Grammar of Assent.*

60. Ward, *Rational Theology,* 109–11.

61. Michael J. Langford, *A Liberal Theology for the Twenty-First Century: A Passion for Reason* (Aldershot: Ashgate, 2001).

62. See Patrick Corcoran (ed.), *Looking at Lonergan's Method* (Dublin: Talbot Press, 1975), 98.

63. Thomas F. Torrance, *God and Rationality* (Oxford: Oxford University Press, 1971).

CHAPTER 3   THE APPEAL TO HISTORY I: THE HISTORY OF RELIGIONS

1. Joseph Butler, *The Analogy of Religion,* ed. J. H. Bernard (London: Macmillan, 1900), 221 (Part II, ch. 7, para. 2).

2. William Alston, *Perceiving God: The Epistemology of Religious Experience* (Ithaca, NY: Cornell University Press, 1991). (see ch. 2, n. 33).

3. Ninian Smart, *Reasons and Faiths: An Investigation of Religious Discourse, Christian and Non-Christian* (London: Routledge & Kegan Paul, 1958), ch. 3.

4. Richard Swinburne, *The Existence of God* (Oxford: Clarendon Press, 1979; rev. edn. 1991), ch. 13.

5. Austin Farrer, *Faith and Speculation: An Essay in Philosophical Theology* (London: Adam & Charles Black, 1967).

6. R. C. Zaehner, *Our Savage God* (London: Collins, 1974).

7. A. E. Taylor, *The Faith of a Moralist*, 2 vols. (London: Macmillan and Co., 1930).

8. Ibid. i. 250.

9. Austin Farrer, 'A Moral Argument for the Existence of God', in Austin Farrer, *Reflective Faith: Essays in Philosophical Theology* (London: SPCK, 1972), 114–33.

10. George Mavrodes, 'Religion and the Queerness of Morality', in Robert Audi and William J. Wainwright (eds.), *Rationality, Religious Belief, and Moral Commitment: New Essays in the Philosophy of Religion* (Ithaca, NY, and London: Cornell University Press 1986), 213–26.

11. Ibid. 225.

12. G. E. M. Anscombe, *Ethics, Religion and Politics: Collected Philosophical Papers*, iii (Oxford: Basil Blackwell, 1981), 26–42.

13. Robert Merrihew Adams, *Finite and Infinite Goods: A Framework for Ethics* (New York: Oxford University Press, 1999).

14. Patrick Sherry, *Spirit and Beauty: An Introduction to Theological Aesthetics* (Oxford: Clarendon Press, 1992).

15. Brian Hebblethwaite, *The Ocean of Truth: A Defence of Objective Theism* (Cambridge: Cambridge University Press, 1988), 110.

16. Wolfhart Pannenberg, *Systematic Theology, i* (Edinburgh: T. & T. Clark 1991), 149.

17. G. W. F. Hegel, *Lectures on the Philosophy of Religion*, ed. P. Hodgson, 2 vols. (Los Angeles: University of California Press, 1988).

18. Friedrich Schleiermacher, *The Christian Faith* (Edinburgh: T. & T. Clark, 1928), ch. 1.

19. Ernst Troeltsch, *The Absoluteness of Christianity and the History of Religions* (London: SCM Press, 1972).

20. Ibid. 112, my emphasis.

21. Ernst Troeltsch, *Christian Thought: Its History and Application* (London: University of London Press, 1923), 3–35.

22. Ninian Smart, *Beyond Ideology: Religion and the Future of Western Civilisation* (London: Collins, 1981).

23. John A. T. Robinson, *Truth is Two-Eyed* (London: SCM Press, 1979).

24. John Hick, *An Interpretation of Religion: Human Responses to the Transcendent* (London: Macmillan, 1989).

25. John V. Taylor, 'The Theological Basis of Interfaith Dialogue', in John Hick and Brian Hebblethwaite (eds.), *Christianity and Other Religions* (London: Collins, 1980), ch. 11.

26. Hick, *An Interpretation of Religion*, ch. 2.

27. Alvin Plantinga, *Warranted Christian Belief* (New York: Oxford University Press, 2000), ch. 2.

28. Ibid. 62 ff.

29. Ibid. 436–57.

30. Alston, *Perceiving God*, ch. 7.

31. Ibid. 270.

32. Adams, *Finite and Infinite Goods*, 367.

33. Ibid. 370.

34. Bernard Williams, *Ethics and the Limits of Philosophy* (London: Fontana Paperbacks and William Collins, 1985), 33.

35. Adams, *Finite and Infinite Goods*, 371.

36. Ibid. 372.

37. See Hans Küng, *A Global Ethic for Global Politics and Economics* (London: SCM Press, 1997).

38. H. H. Farmer, *Revelation and Religion: Studies in the Theological Interpretation of Religious Types* (London: Nisbet & Co., 1954).

39. Ibid. 24.

40. Ibid. 195 f.

CHAPTER 4   THE APPEAL TO HISTORY II: CHRIST
AND THE CHURCH

1. Norman Kretzmann, *The Metaphysics of Theism: Aquinas's Natural Theology in Summa Contra Gentiles I* (Oxford: Clarendon Press, 1997).

2. H. H. Farmer, *Revelation and Religion: Studies in the Theological Interpretation of Religious Types* (London: Nisbet & Co., 1954), 19 f.

3. Alvin Plantinga, *Warranted Christian Belief* (New York: Oxford University Press, 2000), 419 f.

4. Michael Dummett, 'The Impact of Scriptural Studies, in Eleonore Stump and Thomas P. Flint (eds.), *Hermes and Athena: Biblical Exegesis and Philosophical Theology* (Notre Dame, Ind.: University of Notre Dame Press, 1993), 19.

5. A. O. Dyson, *The Immortality of the Past* (London: SCM Press, 1974).

6. Ibid. 23.

7. I. T. Ramsey, *On Being Sure in Religion* (London: University of London, Athlone Press, 1963).

8. Basil Mitchell, *Faith and Criticism* (Oxford: Clarendon Press, 1994).

9. D. Z. Phillips, *Faith after Foundationalism* (London: Routledge, 1988), 9 f.

10. Austin Farrer, *Faith and Speculation: An Essay in Philosophical Theology* (London: Adam & Charles Black, 1967).

11. Ibid. 97.

12. Ibid. 102.

13. Ibid. 103.

14. S. T. Coleridge, *Confessions of an Inquiring Spirit*, repr. from 3rd edn. of 1853, ed. H. St J. Hart (London: Adam & Charles Black, 1956), 42.

15. Basil Mitchell, *The Justification of Religious Belief* (London: Macmillan, 1973), 153 f.
16. David Brown, *Tradition and Imagination: Revelation and Change* (Oxford: Oxford University Press, 1999).
17. David Brown, *Discipleship and Imagination: Christian Tradition and Truth* (Oxford: Oxford University Press, 2000).
18. Norman Whybray, 'Shall Not the Judge of all the Earth Do What Is Just?', in David Penchansky and Paul L. Redditt (eds.), *Shall Not the Judge of All the Earth Do What Is Right? Studies on the Nature of God in Tribute to James L. Crenshaw* (Winona Lake, Ind.: Eisenbrauns, 2000), 1–19.
19. S. Kierkegaard, *Fear and Trembling* (Danish original, 1843), Problemata, Problem I. See the perceptive discussion of these matters in Robert Merrihew Adams, *Finite and Infinite Goods: A Framework for Ethics* (New York: Oxford University Press, 1999), ch. 12.
20. Leopold von Ranke, *The Secret of World History: Selected Writings on the Art and Science of History*, ed. Roger Wines (New York: Fordham University Press, 1981), 21.
21. Richard J. Evans, *In Defence of History* (London: Granta Books, 1997), 17.
22. Brian Hebblethwaite, *Ethics and Religion in a Pluralistic Age* (Edinburgh: T. & T. Clark, 1997), 106.
23. Walter M. Abbott, SJ (ed.), *The Documents of Vatican II* (London and Dublin: Geoffrey Chapman, 1966), 664.
24. James Barr, *The Concept of Biblical Theology: An Old Testament Perspective* (London: SCM Press, 1999).
25. *The Times*, Saturday, 3 Nov. 2001.
26. E. P. Sanders, *The Historical Figure of Jesus* (London: Allen Lane, The Penguin Press, 1993).
27. Ibid. 280.
28. Wolfhart Pannenberg, *Systematic Theology*, ii (Edinburgh: T. & T. Clark, 1994), 356–9.

29. David Brown, *The Divine Trinity* (London: Duckworth, 1985), 101.
30. Ibid. 107.
31. Dummett, 'Impact of Scriptural Studies', 8.
32. For Brown's magisterial response to his critics, Kenneth Surin and Nicholas Lash, see his article 'Wittgenstein and the Wittgensteinians', *Modern Theology* 2 (1985/6), 257–76.
33. Richard Swinburne, *The Christian God* (Oxford: Clarendon Press, 1994), ch. 10.
34. Austin Farrer, *Saving Belief: A Discussion of Essentials* (London: Hodder & Stoughton, 1964), 111–12.
35. Richard Swinburne, *The Resurrection of God Incarnate* (Oxford: Clarendon Press, 2003), 214.
36. Richard Swinburne, *Revelation: From Metaphor to Analogy* (Oxford: Clarendon Press, 1992), 110 ff.
37. *Swinburne, Christian God*, 221 ff.
38. J. Houston, *Reported Miracles: A Critique of Hume* (Cambridge: Cambridge University Press, 1994).
39. Plantinga, *Warranted Christian Belief*, 285.
40. Keith Ward, *Divine Action* (London: Collins, 1990), 188 f.
41. David Jenkins, *God, Miracle and the Church of England* (London: SCM Press, 1987), 5.
42. Farrer, *Saving Belief*, 83.
43. Brown, *Divine Trinity*, 122–6; Swinburne, *Christian God*, 233–5.
44. Keith Ward, *Evidence for the Virgin Birth* (Oxford: Mowbray, 1987).
45. Pannenberg, *Systematic Theology*, ii. 356–9.

CHAPTER 5   A CASE FOR INCARNATIONAL AND TRINITARIAN BELIEF

1. Keith Ward, *Religion and Revelation* (Oxford: Clarendon Press, 1994); *idem, Religion and Creation* (Oxford: Clarendon Press,

1996); *idem, Religion and Human Nature* (Oxford: Clarendon Press, 1998); *idem, Religion and Community* (Oxford: Clarendon Press, 2000).

2. Alvin Plantinga, 'Christian Philosophy at the End of the 20th Century', in James F. Sennett (ed.), *The Analytic Theist: An Alvin Plantinga Reader* (Grand Rapids, Mich.: William B. Eerdmans, 1998), 328–52.

3. Austin Farrer, *Faith and Speculation: An Essay in Philosophical Theology* (London: Adam & Charles Black, 1967).

4. William Alston, *Perceiving God: The Epistemology of Religious Experience* (Ithaca, NY: Cornell University Press, 1991).

5. Alvin Plantinga, *Warranted Christian Belief* (New York: Oxford University Press, 2000).

6. Patrick Sherry, *Spirit and Beauty: An Introduction to Theological Aesthetics* (Oxford: Clarendon Press, 1992).

7. Ninian Smart, *The Concept of Worship* (London: Macmillan, 1972).

8. See e.g. Jürgen Moltmann, *The Coming of God: Christian Eschatology* (London: SCM Press, 1996).

9. See pp. 41f above.

10. Wolfhart Pannenberg, *Systematic Theology*, 3 vols. (Edinburgh: T. & T. Clark, 1991, 1994, and 1998).

11. David Brown, *The Divine Trinity* (London: Duckworth, 1985).

12. Thomas V. Morris, *The Logic of God Incarnate* (Notre Dame, Ind.: Notre Dame University Press, 1986), and *idem*, 'The Metaphysics of God Incarnate', in Ronald J. Feenstra and Cornelius Plantinga, Jr. (eds.), *Trinity, Incarnation, and Atonement: Philosophical and Theological Essays* (Notre Dame, Ind.: University of Notre Dame Press, 1989), 110–27.

13. Richard Swinburne, *The Christian God* (Oxford: Clarendon Press, 1994).

14. See Brian Hebblethwaite, 'Jesus Christ—God and Man: The Myth and Truth Debate', in William R. Farmer (ed.), *Crisis in*

Christology: Essays in Quest of Resolution (Livonia, Mich.: Dove Booksellers, 1995), 1–12.

15. Karl Barth, *Church Dogmatics*, III 2 (Edinburgh: T. & T. Clark, 1960), 231–42.

16. Brown, *Divine Trinity*, ch. 7.

17. Swinburne, *Christian God*, ch. 8.

18. On Richard of St Victor see Edmund J. Fortman, *The Triune God: A Historical Study of the Doctrine of the Trinity* (London: Hutchinson, 1972), 191–4.

19. Ward, *Religion and Creation*, 321–9.

20. Eleonore Stump, 'Atonement according to Aquinas', in Thomas V. Morris (ed.), *Philosophy and the Christian Faith* (Notre Dame, Ind.: University of Notre Dame Press, 1988), 61–91, and *idem*, 'Atonement and Justification', in Feenstra and Plantinga Jr. (eds.), *Trinity, Incarnation and Atonement*, 178–209.

21. Richard Swinburne, *Responsibility and Atonement* (Oxford: Clarendon Press, 1989).

22. On all this see B. L. Hebblethwaite, 'Does the Doctrine of the Atonement Make Moral Sense?', in his *Ethics and Religion in a Pluralistic Age* (Edinburgh: T. & T. Clark, 1997), 77–93.

23. Vernon White, *Atonement and Incarnation: An Essay in Universalism and Particularity* (Cambridge: Cambridge University Press, 1991).

24. J. R. Lucas, 'Reflections on the Atonement', in Alan G. Padgett (ed.), *Reason and the Christian Religion: Essays in Honour of Richard Swinburne* (Oxford: Clarendon Press, 1994), 265–75.

25. Athanasius, *On the Incarnation of the Word of God*, para. 54. In Athanasius, *Contra Gentes* and *De Incarnatione*, ed. and trans. Robert W. Thompson (Oxford: Clarendon Press, 1971), 269.

26. See John Polkinghorne, *Science and Christian Belief* (London: SPCK, 1994), 165 f.

27. Pierre Teilhard de Chardin, *The Phenomenon of Man*, Eng. trans. (London: Collins, 1959).

28. Moltmann, *Coming of God*.
29. See John B. Cobb, Jr, 'What is the Future?', in Ewart H. Cousins (ed.), *Hope and the Future of Man* (Philadelphia: Fortress Press, 1972), 1–14.
30. See Wolfhart Pannenberg, 'Future and Unity', in Cousins (ed.), *Hope and the Future of Man*, 60–77.
31. Brian Hebblethwaite, *The Christian Hope* (Basingstoke: Marshall, Morgan & Scott, 1984).

CHAPTER 6   THE APPEAL TO HISTORY III: UNIVERSAL HISTORY

1. Austin Farrer, *Faith and Speculation: An Essay in Philosophical Theology* (London: Adam & Charles Black, 1967), ch. 3.
2. John Hick, 'Eschatological Verification Revisited', in John Hick, *Problems of Religious Pluralism* (London: Macmillan, 1985), 110–28.
3. See Richard J. Evans, *In Defence of History* (London: Granta Books, 1997), 17.
4. Herbert Butterfield, *Christianity and History* (London: G. Bell and Sons Ltd., 1954), 66.
5. Austin Farrer, 'Double Thinking', in Austin Farrer, *A Celebration of Faith* (London: Hodder & Stoughton, 1970).
6. See Grace Jantzen, *Julian of Norwich: Mystic and Theologian* (London: SPCK, 1987).
7. Trevor Beeson, *Rebels and Reformers: Christian Renewal in the Twentieth Century* (London: SCM Press, 1999).
8. Helmut Gollwitzer, Käthe Kuhn, and Reinhold Schneider (eds.), *Dying We Live: Letters Written by Prisoners in Germany on the Eve of Execution* (Glasgow: William Collins Ltd, 1958).

9. Stanley Hauerwas, *A Community of Character: Toward a Constructive Christian Social Ethic* (Notre Dame, Ind.: University of Notre Dame Press, 1981).

10. Stanley Hauerwas, *The Peaceable Kingdom: A Primer in Christian Ethics* (London: SCM Press, 1983).

11. See Stanley Hauerwas, *Christian Existence Today: Essays on Church, World and Living In Between* (Durham, NC: The Labyrinth Press, 1988), introduction.

12. Stanley Hauerwas, *With the Grain of the Universe: The Church's Witness and Natural Theology* (Grand Rapids, Mich.: Brazos Press, 2001).

13. John Howard Yoder, 'Armaments and Eschatology', *Studies in Christian Ethics* 1 (1988), 58.

14. Hendrikus Berkhof, *Christ the Meaning of History*, Eng. trans. (London: SCM Press, 1966).

15. Hendrikus Berkhof, *Christian Faith: An Introduction to the Study of the Faith*, Eng. trans. (Grand Rapids, Mich.: William B. Eerdmans Publishing Company, 1979).

16. Ibid. 509.

17. Ibid. 510.

18. Ibid. 512.

19. Oliver O'Donovan, *The Desire of the Nations: Rediscovering the Roots of Political Theology* (Cambridge: Cambridge University Press, 1996).

20. Enda McDonagh, *The Gracing of Society* (Dublin: Gill and Macmillan, 1988).

21. O'Donovan, *The Desire of the Nations*, p. 283.

22. Nicholas Wolterstorff, 'A Discussion of Oliver O'Donovan's *The Desire of the Nations*', *Scottish Journal of Theology* 54 (2001), 87–109.

23. Ibid. 109.

24. Oliver O'Donovan, 'Deliberation, History and Reading: A Response to Schweiker and Wolterstorff', *Scottish Journal of Theology* 54 (2001), 137.

25. Walter Rauschenbusch, *Christianising the Social Order* (New York: The Macmillan Company, 1912), 155.

26. See Reinhold Niebuhr, *An Interpretation of Christian Ethics* (London: SCM Press, 1936).

27. Pope John Paul II, *Centesimus Annus* (London: Catholic Truth Society, 1991).

28. Owen Chadwick, *The Secularisation of the European Mind in the Nineteenth Century* (Cambridge: Cambridge University Press, 1975).

29. Eberhard Jüngel, 'The Gospel and the Protestant Churches of Europe: Christian Responsibility for Europe from a Protestant Perspective', *Religion, State and Society* 21 (1993), 141 f.

30. Aloysius Pieris, SJ, *An Asian Theology of Liberation* (Maryknoll, NY: Orbis Books, 1988).

31. Kosuke Koyama, *Waterbuffalo Theology* (London: SCM Press, 1974), and *idem, Three Mile an Hour God* (London: SCM Press, 1979).

32. See Benarsidas Chaturvedi and Marjorie Sykes, *Charles Freer Andrews: A Narrative* (London: George Allen & Unwin Ltd., 1949).

33. Grace Davie, *Europe: The Exceptional Case: Parameters of Faith in the Modern World* (London: Darton, Longman & Todd, 2002).

34. Wolfhart Pannenberg, *Faith and Reality* (London: Search Press, 1977), 120.

35. Grace Davie, Robin Gill, and Stephen Platten (eds.), *Christian Values in Europe* (Cambridge: Christianity and the Future of Europe, 1993).

36. Wolfhart Pannenberg, *Systematic Theology*, iii (Edinburgh: T. & T. Clark, 1998), 525.

37. Onora O'Neill, *A Question of Trust: The BBC Reith Lectures 2002* (Cambridge: Cambridge University Press, 2002).

38. Samuel P. Huntington, *The Clash of Civilizations and the Remaking of the World Order* (London: Simon & Schuster UK Ltd., 1997).

39. J. M. Roberts, *The Triumph of the West* (London: British Broadcasting Corporation, 1985).

40. Francis Fukuyama, *The End of History and the Last Man* (London: Hamilton, 1992).

41. Huntington, *Clash of Civilizations*, 78.

42. See John Coleman Bennett, *Christian Ethics and Social Policy* (New York: C. Scribner's Sons, 1946).

43. Ronald Preston, *Confusions in Christian Social Ethics: Problems for Geneva and Rome* (London: SCM Press, 1994).

44. W. Montgomery Watt, *Islam and Christianity Today: A Contribution to Dialogue* (London: Routledge & Kegan Paul, 1983).

45. Wilfred Cantwell Smith, *Questions of Religious Truth* (London: Victor Gollancz Ltd., 1967).

46. Kenneth Cragg, *The Mind of the Qur'an: Chapters in Reflection* (London: George Allen & Unwin Ltd., 1973).

47. Huntington, *Clash of Civilizations*, 196 f.

48. Hans Küng and Helmut Schmidt (eds.), *A Global Ethic and Global Responsibilities: Two Declarations* (London: SCM Press Ltd., 1998).

49. Huntington, *Clash of Civilizations*, 196.

50. Karl Barth, *Fragments Grave and Gay* (Glasgow: William Collins' Sons & Co., 1971), 30.

51. Huntington, *Clash of Civilizations*, 196–208.

52. Wolterstorff, 'Deliberation, History and Reading', 131 ff.

53. Huntington, *Clash of Civilizations*, 312–16.

54. Ibid. 316–320.

55. Küng and Schmidt (eds.), *A Global Ethic*.

56. See Michael Walzer, *Thick and Thin: Moral Argument at Home and Abroad* (Notre Dame, Ind.: University of Notre Dame Press, 1993).

57. Huntington, *Clash of Civilizations*, 318.

58. Ibid. 320.

Select Bibliography

ADAMS, ROBERT MERRIHEW, *Finite and Infinite Goods: A Framework for Ethics* (New York: Oxford University Press, 1999).

ALSTON, WILLIAM, *Perceiving God: The Epistemology of Religious Experience* (Ithaca, NY: Cornell University Press, 1991).

AUDI, ROBERT, and WAINWRIGHT, WILLIAM J. (eds.), *Rationality, Religious Belief, and Moral Commitment: New Essays in the Philosophy of Religion* (Ithaca, NY, and London: Cornell University Press, 1986).

BARR, JAMES, *Biblical Faith and Natural Theology* (Oxford: Clarendon Press, 1993).

BERKHOF, HENDRIKUS, *Christ the Meaning of History*, Eng. trans. (London: SCM Press, 1966).

BROWN, DAVID, *The Divine Trinity* (London: Duckworth, 1985).

—— *Tradition and Imagination: Revelation and Change* (Oxford: Oxford University Press, 1999).

—— *Discipleship and Imagination: Christian Tradition and Truth* (Oxford: Oxford University Press, 2000).

CLARK, STEPHEN, *God, Religion and Reality* (London: SPCK, 1998).

DYSON, A. O., *The Immortality of the Past* (London: SCM Press, 1974).

FARMER, H. H., *Revelation and Religion: Studies in the Theological Interpretation of Religious Types* (London: Nisbet & Co., 1954).

Select Bibliography

—— *Reconciliation and Religion: Some Aspects of the Uniqueness of Christianity as a Reconciling Faith*, ed. and introduced by C. H. Partridge (Lewiston, NY: The Edwin Mellen Press, 1998).

FARRER, AUSTIN, *Saving Belief: A Discusion of Essentials* (London: Hodder & Stoughton, 1964).

—— *Faith and Speculation: An Essay in Philosophical Theology* (London: Adam & Charles Black, 1967).

FEENSTRA, RONALD J., and PLANTINGA, CORNELIUS JR. (eds.), *Trinity, Incarnation, and Atonement: Philosophical and Theological Essays* (Notre Dame, Ind.: University of Notre Dame Press, 1989).

HAUERWAS, STANLEY, *With the Grain of the Universe: The Church's Witness and Natural Theology* (Grand Rapids, Mich.: Brazos Press, 2001).

HEBBLETHWAITE, BRIAN, *The Christian Hope* (Basingstoke: Marshall, Morgan & Scott, 1984).

—— *The Ocean of Truth: A Defence of Objective Theism* (Cambridge: Cambridge University Press, 1988).

—— *The Essence of Christianity: A Fresh Look at the Nicene Creed* (London: SPCK, 1996).

—— *Ethics and Religion in a Pluralistic Age* (Edinburgh: T. & T. Clark, 1997).

HICK, JOHN, *An Interpretation of Religion: Human Responses to the Transcendent* (London: Macmillan, 1989).

HUNTINGTON, SAMUEL P., *The Clash of Civilizations and the Remaking of the World Order* (London: Simon & Schuster UK Ltd., 1997).

LANGFORD, MICHAEL J., *A Liberal Theology for the Twenty-First Century: A Passion for Reason* (Aldershot: Ashgate, 2001).

LUCAS, J. R., *The Freedom of the Will* (Oxford: Clarendon Press, 1970).

MACINTYRE, ALASDAIR, *Whose Justice? Which Rationality?* (London: Gerald Duckworth & Co., 1988).

MACKINNON, D. M., *The Problem of Metaphysics* (Cambridge: Cambridge University Press, 1974).

Select Bibliography

MITCHELL, BASIL, *The Justification of Religious Belief* (London: Macmillan, 1973).

—— *Faith and Criticism* (Oxford: Clarendon Press, 1994).

MORRIS, THOMAS V., *The Logic of God Incarnate* (Notre Dame, Ind.: University of Notre Dame Press, 1986).

O'DONOVAN, OLIVER, *The Desire of the Nations: Rediscovering the Roots of Political Theology* (Cambridge: Cambridge University Press, 1996).

PADGETT, ALAN G. (ed.), *Reason and the Christian Religion: Essays in Honour of Richard Swinburne* (Oxford: Clarendon Press, 1994).

PENELHUM, TERENCE, *Reason and Religious Faith* (Oxford: Westview Press, 1995).

PHILLIPS, D. Z., *Faith after Foundationalism* (London: Routledge, 1988).

PLANTINGA, ALVIN, *God, Freedom and Evil* (London: George Allen & Unwin, 1974).

—— *Warranted Christian Belief* (New York: Oxford University Press, 2000).

POLKINGHORNE, JOHN, *Science and Christian Belief* (London: SPCK, 1994).

PREVOST, ROBERT, *Probability and Theistic Explanation* (Oxford: Clarendon Press, 1990).

SANDERS, E. P., *The Historical Figure of Jesus* (London: Allen Lane, The Penguin Press, 1993).

SEARLE, JOHN R., *The Mystery of Consciousness* (London: Granta Publications, 1997).

SHERRY, PATRICK, *Spirit and Beauty: An Introduction to Theological Aesthetics* (Oxford: Clarendon Press, 1992).

SMART, NINIAN, *The Concept of Worship* (London: Macmillan, 1972).

—— *The Phenomenon of Religion* (London: Macmillan, 1973).

—— *World Philosophies* (London: Routledge, 1999).

STEINER, GEORGE, *Real Presences: Is There Anything In What We Say?* (London: Faber & Faber, 1989).

Select Bibliography

SWINBURNE, RICHARD, *The Existence of God* (Oxford: Clarendon Press, 1979; rev. edn. 1991).

—— *The Evolution of the Soul* (Oxford: Clarendon Press, 1986).

—— *Responsibility and Atonement* (Oxford: Clarendon Press, 1989).

—— *Revelation: From Metaphor to Analogy* (Oxford: Clarendon Press, 1992).

—— *The Christian God* (Oxford: Clarendon Press, 1994).

TEMPLE, WILLIAM, *Nature, Man and God* (London: Macmillan, 1934).

TORRANCE, THOMAS F., *God and Rationality* (Oxford: Oxford University Press, 1971).

TROELTSCH, ERNST, *Christian Thought: Its History and Application* (London: University of London Press, Ltd., 1923).

—— *The Absoluteness of Christianity and the History of Religions* (London: SCM Press Ltd., 1972).

WARD, KEITH, *Rational Theology and the Creativity of God* (Oxford: Basil Blackwell, 1982).

—— *Religion and Revelation* (Oxford: Clarendon Press, 1994).

—— *Religion and Creation* (Oxford: Clarendon Press, 1996).

—— *Religion and Human Nature* (Oxford: Clarendon Press, 1998).

—— *Religion and Community* (Oxford: Clarendon Press, 2000).

WHITE, VERNON, *Atonement and Incarnation: An Essay in Universalism and Particularity* (Cambridge: Cambridge University Press, 1991).

Index

Index

Index

Index

Hauerwas, Stanley, 131–2, 134, 136, 144, 146
Hawking, Stephen, 3,
Hebblethwaite, Brian, 19, 23, 56, 56, 68, 94, 126
Hedley, Douglas, 25
Hegel, Georg Wilhelm Friedrich, 2, 21, 24, 26, 53, 68, 70–1, 125, 129
Heidegger, Martin, 17, 27
Henson, Hensley, 88, 103
Heschel, Abraham, 113
Hick, John, 73–5, 76, 129
Hinduism, 1, 34, 61, 76, 79, 82, 110–11, 113, 141
history, 26, 28, 30, 33, 34, 35, 37, 40, 42, 44, 49, 50–1, 57, 59, ch. 3 *passim*, ch. 4 *passim*, 110, 111, 114, ch. 6 *passim*
history of religions, 29, 30, 42, 50, ch. 3 *passim*, 87, 92–4, 105, 128–9
Hodgson, Peter, 26
hope, 94, 102, 108, 110, 112, 126
Houston, J., 105–6
humanity, 27, 121, 124, 139
human rights, 132, 137, 142, 143–6
Hume, David, 4, 7, 105
Huntington, Samuel, 140–8

identification, 124–5
identity, 141, 143, 146–8
Illingworth, J. R., 27
imagination, 21, 41, 58, 91, 130
immigration, 146–7
immortality, 14, 38, 65
incarnation, 35, 37, 41, 51, 54, 71, 74, 76, 81, 82, 84, 85, 87, 88, 91, 94, 95, 96, 99–104, 105, ch. 5 *passim*, 128–9
infinity, 26, 123
information technology, 4
inspiration, 51, 117, 121

intention, 7, 9, 14, 76, 125
interactionism, 7
Iqbal, Mohammad, 113
Islam, 1, 34, 61, 71, 72, 75, 79, 92, 95, 111, 113, 123, 129, 141, 143, 145, 146
Israel, 50, 75, 82, 86, 90, 93–4, 108, 118, 128–9, 141, 149

Jaspers, Karl, 74
Jenkins, David, 105
Jesus, 35, 41, 42, 50, 71, 72, 75, 87, 90, 94, 95, 97–103, 106, 108, 118–19, 121–2, 126, 130, 149
John Paul II, Pope, 137
joy, 24, 30, 48
Judaism, 1, 34, 61, 66, 69, 70, 71, 72, 82, 92, 93–6, 104, 111, 113, 123, 129
judgement, 58
Julian of Norwich, 130
Jüngel, Eberhard, 137
justice, 134, 135, 145, 147

Kant, Immanuel, 3, 8, 14–16, 18, 19, 26, 53, 58, 66, 75
Keats, 20
Kenny, Anthony, 5
kenosis, 118
kerygma, 101
Kierkegaard, Søren, 92, 101
Kingdom of God, 126, 130, 131–2, 135–7, 140, 141, 144, 146–7, 149
knowledge, 4, 45–6, 67, 105, 115, 118, 119, 121
Kretzmann, Norman, 86
Küng, Hans, 28, 81, 145, 147

Langford, Michael, 58
language, 9, 11, 14, 17–18
Latin America, 141, 142
law, 93

179

Index

Index

Index

religion (*continued*)
107, 108, 111, 113, 115, 127,
139–40, 141, 146, 148
religious pluralism, 73–5, 76, 77, 96
reparation, 124
repentance, 124
responsibility, 14, 145
resurrection, 35, 39, 50, 51, 85, 97,
98, 99, 100–1, 103–4, 106–7,
120, 149
revealed theology, 33–6, 39–40,
42–3, 46, 50, 55, 57, 59, 61, 65,
76, 83, 110, 115, 127
revelation, ch. 2 *passim*, 60, 65, 67,
68–9, 76, 79, 80, 81, 86, 88, 90–1,
93, 95, 99, 100–1, 105, 110–13,
115, 121, 123, 124, 126, 128
Richard of St Victor, 122–3
Ritschl, Dietrich, 43
Roberts, J. M., 141
Robinson, John, 73
Romanticism, 21
Russell, Bertrand, 6, 25, 65–6, 76

Sacks, Jonathan, 96
sacrament, 121
saints/sanctity, 30, 67, 79, 80, 121,
130, 149
salvation, 39, 81, 95, 101, 108, 112,
124, 129
sanctification, 109, 128, 132–3, 136,
140, 149
Sanders, E. P., 97–8
Schelling, F. W. J., 21, 26
Schleiermacher, Friedrich, 71
Schopenhauer, Arthur, 21
Schubert, Franz Peter, 22
science, 2, 3, 8–9, 12, 15, 22, 30, 34,
74, 105, 113, 115, 121, 125, 126
scripture, 35, 39, 42, 43, 51, 80, 85,
87, 88, 91–3, 97, 113
Searle, John, 5, 7, 10
sectarianism, 131

secularization, 129, 134, 137–8, 141
self, 7–8, 9, 10
sensus divinitatis, 45
Shakespeare, William, 4, 18, 20, 21,
22–4
Sherry, Patrick, 68, 116
Sikhism, 1, 111
sin, 51, 79, 102
sinlessness, 119
Smart, Ninian, 28, 29, 62, 72, 116
Smith, James M., 47
Smith, Wilfred Cantwell, 143
society, 132–3, 135, 140, 142, 149
sociobiology, 3
Sophocles, 18
soteriology, 81, 82, 113, 116, 120,
124
soul, 5, 10
Spinoza, Benedict de, 26
spirit/Spirit, 10, 22, 25, 26, 27, 28,
45, 51, 72, 79, 82, 114, 116, 125,
126, 128, 132, 133, 149
spirituality, 30, 72, 78, 85, 115, 116
state, the, 136, 137, 138, 141, 147
Steiner, George, 20, 21–4, 27
Stoicism, 66
Strawson, P. F., 2–3, 24
Stump, Eleonore, 124
subjectivity, 7–8, 70, 119
substance, 10,
Swinburne, Richard, 5, 10, 32, 47,
50, 54, 63, 86, 89, 98, 101–2,
106–7, 118, 120, 122–3

Taoism, 75
Taylor, A. E., 27, 64–5
Taylor, Charles, 26
Taylor, John V., 74
Teilhard de Chardin, Pierre, 12, 126
teleological arguments, *see* design
arguments
teleology, 16, 57
Temple, William, 27, 88, 103

Index